AMERICAN ABRACADABRA

AMERICAN ABRACADABRA

A Personal Perspective on the March 2016
USA Presidential Primaries and Caucuses

M. O. ENE

Reedbuck

Reedbuck, Inc.
reedbuck@aol.com

ISBN-13: 978-1725617346

ISBN-10: 172561734X

Printed in the United States of America

Those who have shame

Where you live,
There you thrive.

FROM THE AUTHOR

Sunday morning, March 11, 2018, I was watching television news on mute mode. Clocks had sprung an hour forward; officially, the spring was a week away. President Donald J. Trump still headlined. I remote-raised the volume. It was as if time stood still. Mr. Trump was back to the same scene and mode of March 2016 campaigns.

The previous day, Trump was in Moon Township, Pennsylvania. It was a rally to boost the campaign fortunes of Republican Rick Saccone, who was in a tight race against Democrat Conor Lamb for Pennsylvania's 18th Congressional District, scheduled for Tuesday, March 13. The resignation of Republican Rep. Tim Murphy (over his alleged pressuring of a woman with whom he had an extramarital affair to have an abortion) triggered the special election.

Trump boasted and took credits for getting the North Koreans to talk, for the just-concluded XXIII Olympic Winter Games in PyeongChang, South Korea, for working on Mexico to pay for the border walls—in case we had forgotten. He insulted and mocked perceived threats: CNN and NBC ("fake news"); ex-Speaker Nancy Pelosi ("Liberal"), Senator Elizabeth Warren ("Pocahontas"), Rep. Maxine Waters ("very low IQ"); and he promised Oprah a "painful experience" if she dared to run against him ("I know her weakness")—all women and in March, Women's History Month.

Remarkably, Trump unveiled his campaign slogan for elections 2020. It will not be *'Make America Great Again'* again: ("I already did that")! Maybe someone had also told him that *'maga'* is a Nigerian nickname for eternal naïveté, or a dullard. Trump unveiled a brand-new slogan: *'Keep America Great!'* … and he air-added the exclamation point with great gusto! The act evoked March 11, 2016, the day that Trump's train ran into a wall of protests in Chicago, IL. The disorder reminded America of the violent DNC's 1968 Convention in Chicago.

The 2016 presidential elections saddened or thrilled many citizens when the notable year ended in a surprise win —as in a game. Politics is a game played with tons of tricks. As in such unsure undertakings, the tricksters deploy deceits and lies. They use all anticipatory antics that will win a laugh from an appreciative audience, gain trust dishonestly, and deliver on their original intention: to game the system. The con artist in the play is a politician; the voters are the victims.

The tricks that win the approval of voters are many. Some tricks are illicit; others are on the tacky-tasty borderline. The courts do a good job of controlling the bad brands, but the laws do not keep up with many dubious devices designed to swing voters to one's side. By the time existing laws catch up, some bad tricks grow wings and fly with weighty wins, or become etched in the fabrics of society as a tradition.

I know of no standard book on the tricks of politics. Participants read up on available resources and depend on the expertise of those who spend time analyzing the political processes and projecting how they evolve. This collation of comments from March 2016 shares my personal perceptions of the games that politicians play with a straight face in their pursuit of power. Holding alleged wrongdoers accountable for their actions, as with the Russia investigations, guarantees an orderly society and rejects repeats of gangster games.

Sharing such stories is an empowering process. Often, the stories save someone somewhere from suffering similar situations someday. If this book helps someone to avoid a repeat of the madness of March 2016 in 2020 and beyond, then the effort of sharing these personal perspectives on the politics of American presidential elections is worthwhile. Those who want to gamble on politics must know that no one steps into a sludge and steps out smelling sweet.

MOE

Content

"It always seems impossible until it's done."
~ Nelson Mandela

Prologue

For Forms of Government let fools contest;
whatever is best administered is best.

~ Alexander Pope

Democratic practices are an expensive business; they are more so in these United States. Those who aspire to public offices first focus on raising funds before hatching how to defeat their potential opponents. The reason for running comes later, slightly or solely in line with a political party's policy platform. The 2016 USA presidential primaries, caucuses, and conventions were just a bit different.

Presidential hopefuls test the political water by fishing for potential donors or, since Obama 2008, by setting up well-designed websites and harvesting funds from anyone willing to part with amounts ranging from five dollars to the maximum allowed by the Federal Electoral Commission (FEC), an independent agency that regulates campaign finance.

Money is key.

The three-dollar tax checkoffs do not generate enough cash for the increasingly expensive campaigns, now running into billions of dollars. The extraordinary cost is explicable. America is a big country of diverse demographics and geographies. Reaching all corners of the far-flung federation of states and territories in an election cycle is a daunting task that requires immense fiscal resources, much more than FEC provides.

Fundraising is crucial for campaigns. It made a huge difference in 2008. Senator John McCain buckled midway when his campaign coffers emptied early. To entice back those in his donor lists who had donated, the campaign sent them one-dollar bill each. The ploy worked. McCain became the Republican nominee. On the other end, then-Senator Barack Obama raised so much money he could afford to buy hours of television slots and push his candidacy. It worked too. He won.

Rich politicians also invest their own cash, as did Texas business tycoon Henry Ross Perot in 1992 and in 1996; Governor Willard Mitt Romney in 2012; and New York business mogul Mr. Donald J. Trump in 2016. From town council elections to presidential campaigns, American politics is awash with easy cash. Abused, as in cases that pop up in courts, the cool cash could land an otherwise good politician in jail.

Money alone does not an election make. In 2000, it helped then-Gov. George W. Bush (R-TX). In 2016, ex-Florida Governor John Ellis "Jeb" Bush (R) followed the path that served his big brother, now ex-President Bush. Jeb Bush soaked up so much money that the Republican primary elections were his to win. At some point, I noted that Jeb Bush with Ohio Governor John Kasich (R) would beat whomever the Democrats threw up, probably ex-Secretary of State Hillary Rodham Clinton. On that side of the political podium, the Democratic Party patrons have crowned Clinton as its nominee. The party is waiting for her coronation in Philadelphia, PA. Senator Bernie Sanders (I) is just a keen rainmaker from the left flank wetting Clinton's pre-coronation parade across the country.

The Republicans did not factor the emergence of Mr. Donald J. Trump into serious political calculations. That a political novice could rock the Republican Party to its core and, in the process, knock off Jeb Bush from the princely front-runner position was most unlikely. The business world knew Trump very well; but, to the political world, he was a nonstarter.

Why do some candidates do well and others fail? Politics is not an exact science, but it is a science of sorts, full of mean mischiefs and misgivings manufactured in molds of mendacities. Politicians lie loudly and often get away with it. *Politricks* is another name for politics; it tracks tricks and troubles in the electoral processes.

The American primary process is complex. I have learnt a lot lately, and I am still learning. I am in the same situation as some of those running for the highest office in this election cycle. It is no wonder all the candidates hurry to hire highly paid operatives who can rake in cash and plot policies that play to the gallery. Other associates comb the gutters for any scandals the campaigns can use effectively against the other candidates without a bad blowback.

The most important hires of candidates in any presidential election are those who know the rules of the political game. These are battle-tested veterans who have visible scars and fitting hats. Lucky are those candidates who find the David Axlerods (for Obama 2008 and 2012) and Steve Schmidts (for McCain 2008). Candidates who pitch amateur operatives against such revered masters of the game draft a recipe for failure. Good campaign managers are rare, even in a country with two centuries of democratic processes.

This is 2016. Not many things have changed since Republican candidate Abraham Lincoln hired one of the best campaign managers in history, a fellow named David Davis. Lincoln did not have to lift a finger, let alone stick one in the dirt. Davis and his team made the 1860 nomination of Lincoln possible. They spared their principal the shenanigans of political jiggery-pokery and played all cards at the contested convention floor in Chicago, IL. Watching a dramatization of the 1860 Convention in a CNN docudrama, I understood why a lawyer, whom President Lincoln elevated to the lordly position of associate justice of the United States Supreme Court, elected to serve in the Senate in 1877: There was too much political plasma in his blood!

Political operatives understand the nature of political parties, how to succeed against all odds. The first thing to note is that the parties are not answerable to any government body, as long as they are lawful. They are private clubs controlled by diverse influence peddlers, major moneybags, political elites, and power mongers. The floor members are puppets on a stick dancing to a carefully choreographed order of business built on cliquish circles of us-against-them.

The often undefined "them" and "us" depend on the political wind blowing in a certain state, or it may be a divisive national issue. A good example of changing alliances is the fact that the Republican Party formed in 1854 to stop the westward expansion of slavery, and it eventually gave all African Americans the full rights of citizenship. One hundred and fifty years later, African Americans crushingly support the Democratic Party, which was against freeing the slaves of the South!

Following the presidential primaries closely and comparing them with previous primaries prove beyond doubts that both parties are looking for candidates who will win in the November elections. The rules appear to be fluid. Sometimes, subtle changes help to engineer the emergence of a favored candidate. The processes have evolved to become more democratic, but the party bosses and members of the governing bodies still have enormous powers nationally and at state levels.

The two major parties have different guidelines for choosing delegates for the national convention. One thing worthy of note is that the Democratic National Committee (DNC) does not allow a winner-takes-all for any state; it has a system of allocating delegates. The Republican National Committee (RNC) has different rules. 'Different strokes for different states' does not do justice to the dizzying and diverse directives governing Republican primaries, caucuses, or conventions.

Different states have different rules for elections, whether caucuses or primaries. Some states allow only registered party members to participate in their party's presidential primaries (closed primaries); others permit all registered voters to participate, irrespective of party affiliations (open primaries). Some allow independents to choose a party and vote (mixed). Given the variety of rules that govern the presidential processes of DNC and RNC, it is difficult to explain them properly here. In awarding delegates to the national convention, these two major parties aspire to be fair to all the 50 states of the union as well as Washington, DC, Puerto Rico, and the other island territories of American Samoa, Guam, Northern Mariana Islands, and U.S. Virgin Islands.

The chairperson of the Republican Party is a man with a name straight out of the streets of ancient Rome: Reince Priebus. The Dover, NJ native has a complex task of managing 17 candidates and making sure someone emerges with 1,237 delegates out of over 2,472 to win the nomination. An outright win will make his job easy by avoiding a July contested convention in Cleveland, Ohio. Besides 168 members of the national committee, who are automatic delegates, all the other delegates emerge from caucuses and primaries at state levels. The rules vary: Florida, for example, is a winner-takes-all state. Other states award delegates proportionally by special guidelines. A third exists: a hybrid system that will award all or a large portion of the votes to a candidate who scores significantly higher.

Each state gets at least ten at-large delegates; others get more, awarded according to the strength of the Republican Party in the state: the state votes for the party in the previous elections, the strength of its congressional delegation, and the number of state-elected Republican officials. The Republicans also assign at-large delegates to non-state entities: Washington, DC, Puerto Rico, and the other smaller U.S. territories.

Congresswoman Debbie Wasserman Schultz chairs the Democratic National Committee (DNC). She oversees the allocation of delegates, which is mostly proportional, as long as candidates win 15 percent or more of the votes cast in a primary or caucus. The major difference with RNC is the existence of a large number of 'superdelegates,' unpledged delegates drawn from DNC, Congress, governors, former presidents, and or vice presidents. There are over 700 of them this year!

Introduction

These Americans are so naïve; there is no bait which they will not eagerly swallow if it is only offered them with a friendly smile and sufficiently sugared!

~ Emil Witte[1]

The above assessment of American naïveté by a supercilious German envoy at the crack of last century is not entirely exact. Current views of Americans vary; yet, few contest the depiction of these Americans as arrogant. True or false, perception can be everything. Assuming it is a true, we may ask, *'What is wrong with being proud of one's heritage and harboring a sense of superiority; after all, pride is not prejudice?'* Nothing, if it does not devalue others.

Alas, a whole lot of wrongs has popped up from such silly sense of superiority, a psychological crucible for the creation of cultural chauvinism and all forms of apartheid attitudes and prejudiced policies. However, I believe that allegiance to one's fatherland is patriotism. A friend told me recently why Americans could afford to be as arrogant as they want to be: "The United States of America writes checks to every country on earth; remind me which country writes checks to Americans?" The way he said it was a wee bit pompous, but I found the proclamation profound.

---

[1] From "Oh, These Simple Americans" in Emil Witte (1907) Revelations of a German Attaché: Ten Years of German-American Diplomacy, Leipzig, 1907, Translated from German, New York, 1916, p. 19

American presidential elections have again thrust the country into the branding view of the whole world. Since President George Washington left office without succumbing to the bait of term elongation, elections have been a fierce clash of personalities and principles, a feud among politicians positioning for occupancy of the most powerful political office in the free world. This year, 2016, only time will clarify the intense injection of unstudied dimensions. No matter how the contests end, the story will boil down to the entry of a man from the outside right flank, a New York-based business mogul who has dabbled in part-time politics for publicity and for what he could get from the pros.

No notable pundit saw it coming. Those who reflected on the thought of his running openly laughed it off. Lawrence O'Donnell of MSNBC's *The Last Word* gloated endlessly that he had called it right in 2012. It is no longer a pundit's pun; it is happening, and it is not a laughing matter. Mr. Donald John Trump may not be a laughing jackass freely flashing a "friendly smile," but he is offering a new and different political porridge that is both supersoft and "sufficiently sugared."

So many grassroots Republican rebels across the sociopolitical spectrum are swallowing the easy baits, lapping it up, enjoying it free-of-charge, and asking few questions. Mr. Donald Trump's branding brilliance and parochial populism have taken the Republican patrons by a steep surprise. We may have had such an outsider candidate before, but Trump is a different kettle of fish. He is not spending much money on campaigns, and the media houses feed him to Americans as if he is what political pundits and social scientists recommend.

If this presentation appears to be more about Mr. Trump than the other candidates in 2016 presidential primary elections, it is because he is the vortex of the volcano of the primaries. No one is untouched by the sticky splash of yet-to-be-properly-defined *Trumpism*. From the venerable Dalai Lama and Pope Francis, through President Barack Obama and on to almost all contestants in these 2016 presidential primaries, Trump has touched them all with his brash branding and mischievous mendacities. Ordinary citizens who want no part of party politics, who will normally mind their businesses until after partisan politics has weeded out wannabes down to the traditional two nominees, find themselves sucked into the Trump twist.

I was one of those who took Trump's presidential run as a "*yooge* joke," as Trump himself would say. He had toyed with the idea for many moons. He first raised the possibility in an interview with Oprah Winfrey in 1988 and with Larry King for 2000. In 2012, he inched closer to taking the plunge, especially with Tea Party supporters sucking sweetly on his birther-bait lollipop. Then came the 2011 White House Correspondents' Dinner. Seth Meyers, now the host of *The Late Show* on NBC, hosted the shebang. As if Obama had not beaten up Trump enough with his snide and straight jokes, Meyers proceeded to roast Trump like a big fat duck:

> Trump said he's running as a Republican. Which is surprising: I just assumed he was running as a joke ... Trump owns the Miss USA Pageant, which is great for Republicans because it will streamline the search for a vice president ... Trump said recently he has a great relationship with 'the blacks.' Unless the Blacks are a family of white people, I bet he's mistaken.

Trump sat stone-faced throughout the jabs from both Barack Obama and Seth Meyers. He would later lash out at Seth, as was usual with him: "Seth has no talent. He fell totally flat. In fact, I thought Seth's delivery was so bad that he hurt himself." Let us give it to Trump that Seth Meyers' delivery was not the best; it was a bit rushed, but he has talents. That he now hosts *The Late Show* speaks volumes.

On POTUS Obama, Trump had nothing to offer because Obama did release the long form of his birth certificate, thereby silencing Trump's false claims on the issue permanently as a big fat lie. Trump staked so much on proving that Obama was born in Kenya. For an artful dealmaker who boasts of winning always, Trump lost badly. That night sealed any lingering hope for a race to the White House, to which Obama alluded in his spoofs. Trump lost a great chance to shine: He was 64, and there was no political giant on his way but former Governor Mitt Romney (R-MA).

I disagree with the thesis that Trump decided to run for the presidency in 2016 because of the *roast* in 2011. On the contrary, Obama shut down his testing of the water on the same night he sent Special Forces to hunt down Osama bin Laden. On both strikes, Obama succeeded. I doubt Mr. Trump dreamed thereafter of reaching this height in politics. If he did, then he must be the best strategist in modern political history. Trump plays to win. With the money to fund the fun, the sky is no limit. He has chosen to appeal to *"Tommy Tawms"*—the angry white males, many of whom appreciate a man with a beauty-full trophy wife, loads of money, and a jumbo private plane to show off.

Tommy Tawm is not necessarily a raging racist: He is just angry, white, male, and a victim of situations beyond his control. He grew up in a shady school that preached race and religion as all he needed to succeed. He believed in oiled inheritance, in racial entitlements or "white privileges." The election of Obama punctured that cocoon of colored clouds. He can now see clearly that the demography is changing. To succeed, he has to compete with those he considers his inferiors.

Trump has locked these disparate denizens into his dream of becoming the president of USA. They flock to airport hangers and school gymnasia to hear a New York mogul talk casually about economic predicaments, turning tales, and promising to *make America great again.* These people wave at his plane, buy his puerile made-in-China caps and wear them while listening to Trump lambast China for taking their jobs, Mexicans for being rapists, Muslims for coming with evil intentions, and minorities for miscellaneous malfeasance.

The dizzying campaigns have become the basis for all that is wrong with American democracy. Hence, I decided to follow the campaigns for just one month to see how they produce candidates. Since I am stuck at home most evenings and weekends, no thanks to the continued wacky winter, the television and cyberspace provide a laboratory of learning. The social media, especially Twitter, must be the winner of preferred 2016 Internet platform for 'breaking news.' In addition to all the talks about Trump getting millions of dollars in free media coverage, the Twitter people should pay him for promoting the platform more than any individual has done since its creation on March 21, 2006.

German diplomat Witte compares with one of the legendary nine blind men describing an elephant. What he wrote about Americans is relatable and, sincerely speaking, the characteristics may apply to some segments of American civil society. This reality probably informed a meme attributed to a trumped-up Trump's interview in *People Magazine*. In the fake, 1998 interview, Trump supposedly bragged, *"If I were to run, I'd run as a Republican. They're the dumbest group of voters in the country. They believe anything on Fox News. I could lie and they'd still eat it up. I bet my numbers would be terrific."* Well, Trump now says worse things about his Republican supporters nearly 20 years later!

No one should paint people with a broad brush. Groups make mistakes and learn from their missteps. Celebrated British Prime Minister Winston Churchill saw Americans with two naked eyes and conjectured, "You can always count on Americans to do the right thing—after they've tried everything else." The America that chose Barack H. Obama in 2008 will make a choice from the offerings of 2016 and later right any wrong.

Just so we do not forget "everything else" that we will try before doing "the right thing," I will follow the primaries for one month, during which many of the continuing contestants will drop off and narrow the crowded field of wannabes. This is a snapshot story of observations and personal perspectives on the March 2016 events as they unfold, and comments on the political spring storms before the fall presidential tsunami. In the process of making sense of some events, I will revisit history heard, lived, read, or seen.

Enjoy.

1

A March of Madness

Today is Tuesday, March 1, 2016—the so-called "Super Tuesday" in the presidential primary elections of the United States of America (USA). Dubbed "Decision 2016," the preparations have been buzzing for months. Americans look forward to the change of guards. Alas, it is beginning to look like elections in third-rate, third-world countries. The level of trash talking and lies among the top contenders in the Republican Party annoys average Americans. It was so vexing I tuned off partially last December. I desired to tune off totally.

How? That is the question. Answer: You cannot!

The news is all over: the ubiquitous television, social media, e-chat forums, in chatting with friends, and in family forums. Political happenings flood text messages and visuals on electronic platforms, especially WhatsApp—through which videos, images, and memes share widely without restraint nor deterrent. Indeed, an Aristotelian tincture of madness exists in the genius of global information technology. No earthling escapes the pervasive political picnic, even if one is in space.

Apropos, Expedition 46 Commander and fellow New Jerseyan Scott Kelly of NASA returned safely from the International Space Station. Astronaut Kelly landed with cosmonauts Mikhail Kornienko and Sergey Volkov near Zhezkazgan in Kazakhstan. Kelly and Kornienko set a record of enduring weightlessness for one year. For such a feat that will inform human mission to the planet Mars, the media did not deem it worthy of much converge. That is an indication of the level of the media obsession with the primaries and caucuses of today's harvest of delegates.

In a normal election year, the biggest news of the 2016 election cycle would be Senator Bernard "Bernie" Sanders of Vermont, a self-styled socialist and a *non-Jewish* Jew. The former Independent, now Democratic, senator is 'the man,' as they say! So far, he has raised more money from far more people than Obama in 2008. Sadly, Bernie is not happening tonight. The political firewall that Mrs. Hillary Clinton has built in the south appears impenetrable by Bernie's bazookas.

Even if Senator Sanders does an Obama and wins the Democratic primaries, his being the first Jew to run on top of a major party's ticket will still be eclipsed by the wildfire lit by someone that Senator Marco Rubio described tonight in a Florida-focused flay (as he has been doing all week), as "the greatest con man."

Here Rubio goes again against Donald Trump:
"And two weeks from now, right here in Florida, we are going to send a message loud and clear. We are going to send a message that the party of Lincoln and Reagan, and the presidency of the United States, will never be held by a con artist."

Mr. Donald John Trump, the New York business executive and former Atlantic City, NJ casino mogul, is a man that has defied easy description. He is a man who recognizes a good deal when he sees one, a man who is not shy about sowing in lush lands and walking away with his harvest before the Harmattan. Trump is a man who likes all the good things in life and wants to enjoy all the good things in life. He is boastful, even arrogant. He claims to be a winner… anywhere, anyhow, and all the time. He surely has a good nose for deals, and he has a bestseller to show for it.[2]

Mr. Trump is a fascinating character. He has dabbled in far too many big businesses, with some big bankruptcies in tow. It is difficult to keep track of his trail in business ventures. They range from international real estates to casinos in Atlantic City and Las Vegas, from high-class hotel management to marketing of everything from ties, wine, steak, and on to vodka, and from failed aviation and thriving health management to publishing glossy magazines and books on how to make money—like Trump! He is the same Trump of Miss Universe Organization, the Trump that took on television show business with *The Apprentice* and made millions out of the phrase, "You're fired!" Along the line, he married three times and managed to survive all that the tabloids and haters had to throw at him. His latest venture was into the ivory corridors of academia. He founded Trump University. Authorities in New York have shut down the setup, and some graduates of the seminar-selling setup are suing for fraud.

---

[2] Trump: The Art of the Deal (1987) with Tony Schwartz

In politics, Trump is not your typical American tycoon. He leans Republican on economic issues, but he is somewhat a social democrat. He hates abortion, but he wants people to make the choice. Now that it is no longer politically expedient, he has become pro-life. Mr. Trump will speak his mind whenever he gets the opportunity, no matter who lives in the White House. With Obama, he has spoken a mouthful and at levels of scorn. I do not know how Trump stumbled onto the birther movement, but he became the arrowhead, lying that he had sent people to Hawaii and that they were turning up unbelievable stuff about Obama being born in Kenya and smuggled back to Hawaii. Yeah right! The *clever* woman who flew halfway around the world in 1961 with a baby son, to ensure that he could run for the presidency of USA, somehow forgot to name him "Barry Barmason" or something from the Euro sphere, not African-Semitic Barack Hussein Obama!

Last year, TIME magazine passed on Mr. Trump and chose German Chancellor Angela Merkel as the person of the year. This year, 2016, and at this point, no one is second-guessing *TIME*: Donald Trump is it. No matter what changes between now and November, the telling Trump phenomenon will stay with America and the world for some years to come. Historians, pop psychologists, political scientists, and political pundits will find the appropriate terms to explain how and why Trump came so far so fast. They will figure out how the son of a Scottish-immigrant mother named Mary Anne MacLeod and a first-generation German-American man named Fred Trump raised a son that turned the political culture of America on its head.

2

Continued Crushing of Christie

Governor Christopher James "Chris" Christie of New Jersey is fast looking like a big loser… beside Jeb Bush, of course. Here is the fire-eating fellow projected as the best Republican to beat President Obama in 2012. Recall Ann Coulter's prophesy in a February 2011 speech at the Conservative Political Action Conference (C-PAC): "If we don't run Chris Christie, Romney will be the nominee and we'll lose" to Obama. It happened. Recall also that during the Sandy Storm saga of 2012, the mere embrace of Obama by the supposedly heavyweight New Jersey politician seemingly tilted the election to the President—a 'crime' the Republicans still hold against him.

I will not make a good politician. I hold the view because of the petty principles of politicians that place party above patria. Politicians with the gift of garb are of malleable molds of good salespersons. This explains Trump appeals to ordinary Americans, regardless of his jingoism. Politicians have no shame. They will embrace anything that smells of power without blinking once. Anything that leads to political power smells good.

Last weekend on a tarmac in Tennessee, after Christie had endorsed Trump publicly, Trump told him, "Get on a plane and go home. It's over there. You go home." It was a great advice, albeit crude and rude: Christie had been missing from his home state of New Jersey, and he had become a very unpopular governor. Regardless, this was not a way to treat anyone, let alone an ally governor of a consequential state. It was a slap in the face of Christie. Trump probably did it to teach Cruz and Rubio a lesson on how not to badmouth him—the frontrunner. It seemed as if Trump was saying:

> *My fate cries out*
> *And makes each petty artery in this body*
> *As hardy as the Nemean lion's nerve.*
> *Still am I called. Unhand me, gentlemen.*
> *By heaven, I'll make a ghost of him that lets me.*
> *I say away! Go on, I'll follow thee.*[3]

Tonight, as if feeling sorry for treating Governor Christie crudely and condescendingly, Trump featured him at a news conference, his introduction to becoming a presidential persona in his palatial Palm Beach, FL home, the Mar-a-Lago estate. Christie was a sad sight. He looked lost, as if in a daze. He looked like a man Friday, the chief butler, a man unsure of his political destiny. To juice it, Christie is the national chair of the Republican Governors Association. It was embarrassing and a sore sight, not good to behold. It was so ruthless that throughout the evening New Jerseyans tweeted and asked Christie to resign or face a recall.

---

[3] ~ William Shakespeare, Hamlet, Act 1, Scene 4

I noted the nonstop media sustenance of Trump. They trooped to his house. All the cable news channels were there to cover an unusual post-election press conference in a White House-like environment. Trump did not hide that he watches the big three of cable news (CNN, MSNBC, and Fox). He knew when to appear and soak the airwaves for his own show. He spared none in his trademark loose lambast, not even Speaker Paul Ryan: "Paul Ryan, I don't know him well, but I'm sure I'm going to get along great with him. And if I don't, he's going to have to pay a big price."

Does Trump truly understand how the American system of government works, that Speaker Ryan can initiate impeachment proceedings? Trump was reacting to Ryan's condemnation of his failure to disavow the endorsement of KKK, the supremacist hate group. On the sad situation, Speaker Ryan had posited:

> When I see something that runs counter to who we are as a party and as a country, I will speak up, so today I want to be very clear about something. If a person wants to be the nominee of the Republican Party, there can be no evasion and no games. They must reject any group or cause that is built on bigotry. This party does not prey on people's prejudices. We appeal to their highest ideals.... And if someone wants to be our nominee, they must understand this.

I bet the Speaker will chuckle at the threat, but the Republican Party should take the rise and rise of Mr. Trump seriously. A declared war does not the lame consume. Shifting the early primaries south was not a sound strategy. If Trump sustains the momentum in the South, it will be too late to stop him back up north.

Back to New Jersey Governor Chris Christie, the search for his successor started today, March 1, 2016. Mayor Mark J. Sokolich of Fort Lee, NJ came to mind. His refusal to support Christie's reelection in 2014 allegedly led to Bridgegate, in which Christie's political appointees ordered the blocking of two of three toll lanes from Fort Lee, NJ to George Washington Bridge and caused huge traffic problems. The scandal sapped Christie's popularity coast-to-coast in 2015, though the US attorney office was yet to indict him of wrongdoing.

I woke up this morning, March 2, and I felt like returning to my no-politics mode. Noon, I checked out Barbara Buono. The Essex County native (Newark-born, Nutley-raised) and Middlesex County resident was no longer living in New Jersey. Apparently, after the 2013 loss to Christie and some subsequent legal troubles with state ELEC,[4] the former Democratic majority leader of the state senate sold her home in Metuchen, NJ and moved to Portland, Oregon.

Democratic Assemblyman John S. Wisniewski, who has served the 19th Legislative District in the New Jersey General Assembly since 1996, appears at this point to be a good choice. However, his chairing of Bernie Sanders' campaign in New Jersey is fraught with dangers. The Clintons have the memory of an elephant. I doubt Senator Cory Booker wants to tumble again in the state so soon after leaving for Washington, DC. The door is open for another outsider like Trump. Whoever emerges tops among Democrats in New Jersey will replace Christie. What a difference a year makes!

---

[4] Election Law Enforcement Commission

3

Trump and the Rest of the Field

The Democratic field is already set. There are no surprises from Super Tuesday results. Hillary Clinton's southern strategy is holding strong. Sanders is not too far behind, but it is now obvious that the relationship between the Clintons and the Black community has not waned. Apropos, it looks like Hillary's campaign has sidelined Bill Clinton after Donald Trump made Monicagate an issue and after Bill's lackluster appearances in the New Hampshire primaries. Trump has served an apéritif of campaign slugfest; the main course will come closer to November.

Senator Bernie Sanders has lost the momentum. He will hang in there and cause major headaches, if not heartaches. In the end, Hillary Clinton will clinch the nomination. She is the essence of DNC establishment. Sanders is not really a Democrat. Like Trump, he saw stranded and speechless souls; he stepped up to speak for them. They listened, paid his campaign bills, and cheered him on to national prominence. Unlike Trump's troops, Sanders is burning their money like a drunken sailor chasing ladies of leisure in Las Vegas.

The only field that needs further trimming is the GOP field. I watched *The Rachel Maddow Show* (TRMS), hoping to see her poof Dr. Ben Carson, the celebrated retired neurosurgeon. It is about time the brother got a break from the roadshow that started with 17 aspirants hoping to replace Obama. The renowned medico of *Gifted Hands* fame has given the presidential pursuit his best shot and gathered some steam, but these are not normal Republican presidential primaries. Brother Ben appears not to have had enough of the charade that will "horrify our founding fathers." He plans to stay in the race, according to reports, but he will be a no-show at the next debate.

Interesting!

Dr. Ben Carson is no longer trending. Trump still holds the follow-me wand of magic that attracts media attention as light attracts moths. According to Lawrence O'Donnell of *The Last Word* show on MSNBC, the 30th prominent Republican to vow never to vote for Trump has emerged in Charles Duane "Charlie" Baker IV, the 72nd governor of Massachusetts. Yet, his state voted overwhelmingly for Trump, the frontrunner. Baker took over from Democratic Duval Patrick on January 8, 2015. It is easy to pledge openly not to vote for Trump; but as with all read-my-lips political proclamations, many of these politicians will come later to Trump's table. He will be the party's nominee in July. The only people I am sure will never vote for Trump, regardless of what they say in public, are the Bush people, especially the family. Trump went too far in insulting their matriarch, the much-respected former First Lady Barbara Bush.

If you think political punditries ended with the results of Super Tuesday now widely available, you have not flipped through the monologues of Trevor Noah (*The Daily Show*), Larry Wilmore (*The Nightly Show*), Jimmy Fallon (*The Tonight Show*), Stephen Colbert (*Late Show*) and Jimmy Kimmel (*Jimmy Kimmel Live*). With all the events of yesterday, South African Trevor Noah offloads on the possibility of a President Trump. He starts with Ben Carson's slow exit, Marco Rubio sweating it out, and Ted Cruz misinterpreting and making up numbers. It is brutal humor. Trump is indeed a gift that keeps giving to late-night comedy shows, a fowl that provides the flammable feathers that roast its flesh. With the exception of Governor John Kasich of Ohio, who does not count much in popularity, comedians spare none: Trump, Christie (on whom the state print media issued a common editorial asking him to step down), Paul Ryan, Hillary (*"still feeling the Bern"*) Clinton, and Bernie Sanders himself.

Along the Atlantic seaboard, the cold dawn of March 3 leaked that the Republican stakeholders were no longer waiting for Trump's train to decelerate on its own inertia. *Morning Joe* talk show announced that Mitt Romney (the 70th governor of Massachusetts and the 2012 Republican nominee against President Barack Obama) will offload unpleasantries on Donald Trump. He did. Hear him:

> "Here's what I know: Donald Trump is a phony, a fraud. His promises are as worthless as a degree from Trump University. He's playing members of the American public for suckers: He gets a free ride to the White House, and all we get is a lousy hat."

The surprising speech, in my opinion, was way, way beneath the stature of Governor Mitt Romney. You do not attack a politician for winning; you contrast and take sides, if take a side one must. Romney just wanted to stop Trump; to him, it was anyone but Trump. Yet the same Trump had supported him to the hilt in 2012. Romney knew about Trump's "hallmark dishonesty" in insisting that Obama was born in Kenya and smuggled back to America… long after Obama had released state-sealed and supporting documents showing that he was a 'natural-born American'—whichever way the nation's Supreme Court defines it whenever the case gets there.

Romney knew all about Trump's "bullying, the greed, the showing off, the misogyny, the absurd third-grade theatrics," yet Mitt the Mormon clergy sought Trump's support and relished the endorsement as meaning "a great deal to me." I recall the setting in 2012: right inside Trump's hotel in Las Vegas, Nevada. What changed? No one asked Romney. No one cared.

Mr. Romney was not alone in the stop-Trump-train squad. Increasingly, some prominent politicians of the Republican Party were speaking up against Trump. In a statement, Senator John Sidney McCain, the Republican of Arizona and 2008 GOP nominee against Obama, backed Romney:

> I share the concerns about Donald Trump that my friend and former Republican nominee, Mitt Romney, described in his speech today. I would also echo the many concerns about Mr. Trump's uninformed and indeed dangerous statements on national security issues that have been raised by 65 Republican defense and foreign policy leaders.

Trump shot back at Romney straight from the hips, returning fire for fire: "He was begging for my endorsement. I could have said, 'Mitt, drop to your knees': he would have dropped to his knees." No one goes south with Trump and comes back empty-handed. Going toe-to-toe with Trump leads straight to the sewer. Ask Jeb Bush!

The risqué retort to Romney's rabid roasting came from the same Trump who said of Romney four short years ago: "Mitt is tough, he is smart, he is sharp; he is not going to allow bad things to continue to happen to this country we all love. So Governor Romney, go out and get 'em!" Well, to Republicans against the candidacy of Trump, Romney was doing just that: stopping "bad things" from happening "to this country we all love"!

I keep asking myself why grown men, rich men of famed families, stoop so low and play the dozens with sleazy statements stinking of scarcely shielded sexual suggestions. As with the show-of-hands shame with Marco Rubio, Trump's "dropped to his knees" statement is loaded and probably means what an average person understands: a blowjob! Romney's attack fizzled before the Fox News Debate aired live from Detroit, Michigan at 9 pm EST.

The 11th Republican candidates' debate kicked off with a walk-back of the hilarious but discourteous exchanges of the week. Tonight's debate featured the remaining candidates: Trump, Cruz, Rubio, and Kasich. The stage looked more like a presidential primary, not the crowded setups of late last year.

If the debates were about issues, someone forgot to tell Mr. Donald J. Trump. He was more comfortable with talking about his polling numbers, his winnings, and his great attributes: not-small and "no-problem" body extremities that embarrassed Ms. Megyn Kelly, one of the moderators. Moderator Chris Wallace posed the first challenge to Trump's claims since the verbal scuffle in the CNBC debate.

The debate went south soon after and measured up to the usual trading of insults and bandying of numbers that did not add up. The Fox's moderators were doing a good job this time around. Alas, the invectives, the lack of specificity, and the contemptuous comments flattened the last debate of the four surviving Republican candidates before Super Saturday. It was so easy to turn off television noise from the 100% polemics and 0% policies.

Trump is turning American politics on its head. To him, it appears politics is about pop culture, about saying whatever one wants, allowing the media to chew off whichever part they want most and munch on it, and about staying on the top of all mass media outlets. The media play along with Trump, feeding on whatever he serves in his daily tweets that are never short on the steady supply of tidbits to talk about and analyze annoyingly ad nauseam and apparently ad infinitum. The talking heads do not tire. Some may complain, but they keep watching and talking about Trump's tweets. Watching Trump has become a reality show of sorts. Not like waiting and wondering 'Who killed JR,' but it is close; it is like waiting for something, anything involving Mr. Trump, to happen on live television.

4

Threshing Trump

It was the Summer of Trump
But, are we set for the Fall of Trump
When 'Stump for Trump'
Becomes 'Dump Trump'?[5]
Fall came. Nothing fell apart. The beat boomed. Winter brought no chills. Spring is here and, finally, the Trump train slows down. Though beaten in delegates count yesterday by Ted Cruz, who trumped him in Iowa State, Trump is set to win. Republican leaders are bringing out the slaying swords. The fight to derail or ditch the Trump train is emerging. John McCain and Mitt Romney, the last two Republican nominees, are out on the open field. Senator Lindsey Graham (R-SC) today, Sunday, March 6, 2016, told Chuck Todd on *Meet the Press* that the choice of Cruz or Trump was "death by being shot or poisoning. I'd rather risk losing without Donald Trump than try to win with him because it will do more damage over time."

It is still a long, never-travelled road to Tuesday, November 8!

---

[5] Posted on Facebook wall, Wednesday, 9.9.15

How did Trump train get so far? The story can wait. The truth is that no political pundit saw the train coming so fast and reaching this far. The slowdown starts today, but the contenders for the driver's seat are not the best of the rest. With Trump's Jeb-like "low-energy" visible on television this morning, perhaps due to campaign fatigue, he still makes mincemeat of Cruz and in a way that appeals. In explaining Cruz's win in Maine, Trump reinjects Cruz's citizenship controversy: "I want to congratulate Ted on Maine and on Kansas. And he should do well in Maine because it's very close to Canada. Let's face it, I mean." Vintage Trump. It is still a four-way race, and 'dump Trump' detractors may be emboldened to break their covers.

This Sunday after the so-called Super Saturday of March 5, I look at the Trump's train that has wrecked prominent politicians as it cruises ceaselessly across the country on auto drive. My conclusion is that the train has been waiting at the station for seven years. Trump merely climbed into the driver's seat and took off on a joyride, blaring jingoistic songs that appeal to Tommy Tawms—the angry white males.

Trump is telling tall tales. His folks do not care. They know that he hates no one as much as he claims. They know that he is not going to build walls, even if he uses his own money, which he will not do. Trump does not have the money. Mexico will not pay a paltry peso! Tawms want someone to take and talk the threats of such conservative radio talkshow hosts as Mark Levine, Rush Limbaugh, Sean Hannity, Laura Ingraham, and Michael Savidge to the White House, *denegrofy* it, and make it *white*... sorry, *great* again!

Decision 2016 is full of batshit[6] banters and trash talks. Political insults are not new in the western world. When I arrived in Britain for postgraduate studies, I got a colored television. The first night, Labour Party leader Neil Kinnock was delivering a strong rebuttal to what Prime Minister Margaret Thatcher had said earlier. He called her a liar to her face. I was shocked that such an exchange could happen in the hallowed halls of great British Parliament. There was just a table separating the opposing politicians. They were so close someone could have swung a punch if it were in the Taiwanese or Ukrainian parliament. This was probably why in 2009 USA I was not taken aback, as President Obama visibly was, when Congressman Joe Wilson (R-SC) shouted, "You lie!" at him from his party corner of the chamber. The clear crack in congressional correctness got strong condemnations. It was a small step down the slippery slope of silliness in decorum at the highest level.

I heard on *TRMS* that negative campaigning started after the tenure of George Washington. Thomas Jefferson took it to John Adams: the vice president versus the president. They used surrogates. Jefferson's hacks insulted President Adams as having a "hideous hermaphroditical character, which has neither the force and firmness of a man, nor the gentleness and sensibility of a woman." Adams' proxies retaliated and called Jefferson "a mean-spirited, low-lived fellow, the son of a half-breed Indian squaw, sired by a Virginia mulatto father." *Wait a minute: did America have its first native–American/colored president in Jefferson!*

---

[6] Senator Graham: "My party has gone batshit crazy," after Super Tuesday

Such words as 'fool, hypocrite, criminal, tyrant, weakling, atheist, libertine, coward, and detestable' hauled across the partisan divide. Eventually, from these exchanges emerged the infamous story of President Jefferson fathering the children of his wife's half-black, half-sister Sally Hemings. We sure have an *exemplary* ancestry in political pettiness!

It is therefore surprising that over 200 years later, folks cringe as the presidential candidates huff and puff inside pathetic pots of political pyronomics. Politics is a fierce feud, sometimes physical but typically a war of words. Trump has removed the cover of drudges and surrogates; he is doing the deed himself. He is a bully, no doubt about it. Like all bullies, the best antidote is instant and rabid retaliation. This is what Senator Marco Rubio has done to crawl under Trump's skin. Beyond calling Trump "a con artist," he speculated.

> "He is taller than me; he's like 6' 2", which is why I don't understand why his hands are the size of someone who is 5' 2." Have you seen his hands? And you know what they say about men with small hands–You can't trust them."

The crowd of Rubio supporters knew better! The innuendo is not lost on Trump. He could not ignore the slur that actually refers to the size of his penis. Trump had it coming: referring to the Senator as "Little Marco" is both demeaning and vicious. After South Carolina primaries, Marco Rubio stayed on Trump as white does on *basmati* rice. On Friday, February 26 in Dallas, Texas, Rubio took some time to mock Trump's spelling and social media habits. Last Thursday's night, he went for the kill while flashing his boyish Latino smile.

Rubio alluded that Trump pee-ed on himself at a commercial break during the debate: Trump "went backstage; he was having a meltdown [with] one of those little sweat mustaches." He asked for a full-length mirror. "Maybe to make sure his pants weren't wet."

We now know why the shorthand slight gets at Trump. In 1988, a certain Graydon Carter described him as a "short-fingered vulgarian… just to drive him a little bit crazy." Mr. Carter confirmed on *The Last Word* with Lawrence O'Donnell that Trump kept contesting the claim with him until recently. Rubio walked on hot wires and short-circuited raw nerves. Trump's regular use of such derogatory terms for Rubio as "Once a choker, always a choker," "Mr. Meltdown," "choker," and "clown" shows a man stressing and struggling to square the insult scoreboard. Trump replays how Rubio grabbed a bottle of water during his 2013 response to Obama's State of the Union address.

Rubio has stepped on Trump's toes and lives to tell the story in full… until Florida primaries next week. Others before Rubio were not so lucky. Governor Rick Perry of Texas was the first victim down. Scott Walker of Wisconsin followed. Bobby Jindal of Louisiana hit back so hard at Trump, but he too collapsed. Senator Lindsey Graham (R-SC) folded from the day Trump shared his cellphone number on live television. Then there was Jeb: John Ellis Bush. What "low-energy" Jeb failed to do, Rubio did: fight back. When Donald Trump slighted his mother, former First Lady Barbara Bush, Jeb still pussyfooted with him. Elsewhere, anyone who takes such a swipe at a man's mother *kisses* the ground, minimally, in a symbolic apology to Mother Earth!

Trump probably never believed he would get this far in the presidential primaries. Besides the probably apocryphal urban legend about Bill Clinton egging him into the race to muddle the Republican waters, no one knows what propelled Trump to enter the race on Tuesday, June 16, 2015. Since then he has been railing against Mexico and Mexicans, Muslims, minorities, and political correctness. Take a read:

> When Mexico sends its people, they are not sending their best. They are not sending you. They are not sending you. They are sending people that have lots of problems, and they are bringing those problems with us. They are bringing drugs. They are bringing crime. They are rapists. And some, I assume, are good people.

Trump hangs his rapists slur on the rape of a citizen in California by a deported illegal who found his way back. When ISIS-inspired insurgents went on a killing rampage in Paris, the wide world of civilized citizens cringed and criticized. Trump fed on the horror and opened the door on surveillance of mosques and establishing of a database for all Muslims living in USA. He spiced it up with the unfounded allegation that thousands of Muslims jubilated on rooftops in Jersey City, NJ during the destruction of World Trade Center on 9/11: September 11, 2001. When the mass shooting in San Bernardino, California occurred, Trump called for the barring of all Muslims from entering the United States. On Monday, December 7, 2015, at a rally in South Carolina, he echoed: "Donald J. Trump is calling for a total and complete shutdown of Muslims entering the United States until our country's representatives can figure out what the hell is going on."

"Until we are able to determine and understand this problem and the dangerous threat it poses, our country cannot be the victims of horrendous attacks by people that believe only in Jihad, and have no sense of reason or respect for human life."

Trump does not mask his scorn for Black Lives Matter (BLM) movement. He continues to mock Bernie Sanders for allowing a couple of female BLM activists to take over his microphone, vowing repeatedly that it could never happen to him. As if to make it a certainty, African Americans at his rallies are promptly escorted or forced out by his private security forces and heckling supporters. A known white supremacist led a horde heckling and pushing out a black student. She posed no danger amidst a sea of white male heads.

On February 29, 2016, the campus police at Valdosta State University in Georgia escorted out black students attending a Trump's rally. There was no sign that the students were planning to disrupt the rally, and there was no indication that they were BLM members. Being black and attending Donald Trump's rally was enough evidence for forceful eviction.

Ms. Tahjila Davis recounted the humiliation on her Facebook page:

"After we got our tickets, waited in line, went through security and walked to get our seats, Trump's secret service came up to us and asked us to leave. Again, a group of all black students who WERE NOT there to protest, but to sit in the rally like every[one] else, got KICKED OUT FOR NO REASON. There was no yelling, we held no signs, no nothing. After getting put out, the police continued to try to escort us off of our own campus."

Trump sometimes walks back his steps from the dungeon of detestation. Without a simple apology for previously held views, he lets out how he loves the same group he rails against, such as China, Mexico, minorities, Muslims, Latinos, disabled soldiers (except veterans that were never captured), and women. He finds it difficult to disavow the support of overt white supremacists, including "a bigot, a racist" David Duke whom he vowed not to work with 16 years ago in the Reform Party!

The mainstream media rarely follow up strongly on the inconsistencies of Trump. It is as if Trump has media managers on his payroll, and he is not spending much money on advertisements. On the contrary, Trumps makes money for the media. Only late-night comedians religiously point out the clear contradictions in Trump's alternate universe—for cheap laughs.

The American media are obsessed with Trump. He drives viewership mostly because he appears to be the only thing at the top of television news. A breaking news on old O. J. Simpson's murder case could not take Trump off the top of news and talkshows. He says stuff he has no intention of doing. He knows too well that he is not going to build a 45-foot, 50-foot, or higher walls across the land border with Mexico, let alone get Mexico to pay for it; *build* it, maybe—if he pays them! Trump says it so often it now sounds achievable. Former Mexican President Vicente Fox threw an F-bomb on television in vowing not to pay for the wall: "I'm not going to pay for that f***ing wall. He should pay for it." Trump has demanded an apology; it is yet to come, and I doubt Vicente Fox will oblige.

Why do some succumb to Trump's temptations with no iota of reservation and, on the other end of the spectrum, some suffer from Trump Anxiety Syndrome? Mr. Trump is still a laughing matter in some quarters, but many Republicans are not amused. Some serious-minded Democrats are no longer laughing either. The increasing possibility of a President Donald J. Trump is not a laughing matter.

There will be ample analyses in months and years ahead. Until then, enjoy a fine read from Samuel Joseph Wurzelbacher ("Joe the Plummer" of McCain-Obama rumble in 2008) speaking on MSNBC, probably a previous recording:

> "He's a winner. He's made billions. He's dated beautiful women. His wife is a model. That's not to sniff at. And a lot of people believe he can bring that kind of success to the White House."

On the other end of our political spectrum, pundits and celebrities call Trump names. Some vow to relocate to Canada if he wins. Trevor Noah joked that he was lucky to have an alternative home and welcomed his viewers to South Africa. Extremists relate Trump to Hitler. His own party people call him names: con artist, fraud, fascist, phony, loser, and refer to his hair and other anatomical extremities—private or not. There are TV-political psychologists who offer unprofessional profile diagnoses, calling Trump "egoist," "maniac," and this gem: "nazissistic" (from 'Nazism/narcissistic'). These talking heads often offer trite treatments and point out which traits or utterances disqualify Trump from the presidency of United States.

Comparisons with Nazi's Adolf Hitler are rife. Facebook memes parade crude comparisons, except the execution of Jews. Bloggers trumpet 'character defects, cerebral disturbances, alternate universe,' and such tired expressions that really say little about the triumph of Trump in the Republican presidential primaries. Jeb Bush was wrong: Trump could insult his way to the White House. The earlier serious pundits figure out Trumpism and a cure, the better for those who wish to see the first female president in Hillary Clinton.

Besides both being of paternal Germanic ethnic extraction, floating comparisons with Adolf Hitler may be fantasy, but electing Trump and losing the Senate majority calls for a change on both sides of the ongoing Republican divide: Trump tones down his jingoistic jargons and Republicans back off and stop trying to topple Trump. Trump himself offered an olive branch yesterday afternoon in Wichita, Kansas, by calling on Republicans to give up trying to stop him. "The Republicans are eating their own. They've got to be very careful. We have to bring things together."

The dealmaker and author of *The Art of the Deal*, Trump appears to be showing the way. He followed up this afternoon by asking Marco Rubio to give it up, since there was no path to the top for him, the Puerto Rico win-all aside. This could be a *wink, wink* for VP slot. Thus, in the midst of the country mourning the death on former First Lady Nancy Reagan, who passed earlier today (March 6) at 94, Trump found a way to stay on top of political commentaries. He probably feels the Cruz momentum and fears that the Republicans could find Cruz a less bitter pill to swallow.

No matter how Republican establishment tries to stop the Trump train, either derailed or destroyed politically, Mr. Donald J. Trump looks set to clinch the delegates needed to secure the nomination. If he does not get the required 1,237 delegates, a brokered or contested convention will be difficult to contain. All the loose talks and toilet talks, all the trash talks, will swing to the sorry silos of stories. Talks of drafting Speaker Paul Ryan as a modern messiah merely test the political waters. The unlikely move will be the greatest game changer in the race, but no one can muzzle out Trump at this point. He knows it.

On Saturday, January 23, in Sioux Center, Iowa, Trump talked big: "I could stand in the middle of 5th Avenue [New York City] and shoot somebody, and I wouldn't lose voters." That was then; as of today, the train is cruising at Amtrak speed, not then Acela rapid. Yet, Trump retains an unbeatable attitude that reassures the weakest of supporters. Watching Trump campaign, one gets the sense that he truly does not give a hoot about anything and that the party setup is beneath him!

For the good of the party, for peace and progress, the Republican establishment should allow the process to unfold. If Trump emerges, the party should take the maternal advice of Mother McCain. When asked if the Republican base would accept her son Senator John McCain (R, AZ), a political maverick, as the nominee, she said, "Yes, I think holding their nose they're going to have to take him." It happened, but McCain went on to lose to Obama. The Republicans should take the good advice of Mrs. Roberta McCain, given in January 2008: hold their noses, and take the Trump tablet.

If Trump loses the general election, GOP can sit back and pick up the pieces. If Trump wins, he may be anything but the conservative crusader he has been pretending to be these past few months. By skipping CPAC convention, a conference of conservatives, Trump is signaling that he is more about his big ego, about the name "TRUMP," and about being on top of the moneymaking machine. He seems not to care about taking over the party as-is; on the contrary, he looks like an activist building a personal political base, a parallel movement to the Republican Party. We will never know the political Trump until he gets power. As Abraham Lincoln observed, "Nearly all men can stand adversity, but if you want to test a man's character, give him power."

Trump is like the proverbial lower River Niger tsetse fly that perched on a scrotal boil: hit it, and you may burst the boil; leave it, and it may pollute the pus. The Trump train is an enigma; it could dissolve into thin air down the tracks; or, it could stay the course, crash through belated barricades rolled out hurriedly by the Romneys and the McCains of the Republican Party, and burst out of Cleveland, Ohio in July of 2017 tooting, "Mr. Trump goes to Washington, DC!" Whatsoever the outcome, the good people of these United States will not forget the day that Trump and Melanie floated down the Trump Tower elevator in 2015. A seeming joke has become a serious job!

For now, the train moves on.

5

Hillary v. Bernie

L ast night at the CNN Democratic debate in Flint, Michigan, hosted by Anderson Cooper and Don Lemon, Secretary Hillary Clinton and Senator Bernie Sanders squared off. I still do not get why the Democrats choose weekends to debate. I do not buy the reasons floating around. Folks deserve a big break from politics on Sundays. There are still Blue Law states where you cannot buy alcohol products on Sundays or, at least, until afternoon. Yet, on March 6, 2016, the two Democrats still in the running are debating!

For my evening entertainments, CBS now rules on Sunday evenings. Thus, between watching Canadian Prime Minister Justin Trudeau on *60 Minutes* and two engaging television dramas, *Madam Secretary* and the raunchy drama *The Good Wife*, I managed to watch segments of the debate. One thing I find intriguing is that no one has injected neither gender nor religion in the Democratic field. Former Governor of Maryland Martin O'Malley, 53, never injected age before the two ageing politicians (68 and 73) kicked him to the curb and out of the contest.

Whoever has not made up his or her mind about Clinton or Sanders must have been living in a cave since 2015. Bernie, as fans fondly call Sanders, has made incredible impacts on 2016, starting from "Bernie who?" at 3% to giving the Clintons a 100% run for their ratings and money. However, the Clintons' chain of cohorts is not visibly rattled. Whether you love or loathe the Clintons, one thing is certain: the Democratic Party establishment is not about to deliver the party to an independent, self-proclaimed socialist who chooses only to caucus on the party's side of the political divide.

Nothing more really convinces voters to choose between the two top Democrats. The differences are obvious; they merely rehash them with nuances each time they debate. On guns, trade pacts, Wall Street, campaign financing, and healthcare, the differences are clear. The debates only help Hillary to push Bernie further to the fringe and hope that his frank speak lands him in new hot waters. As she did in South Carolina, pushing Bernie out of Obamasphere, she does it again in Michigan by accusing Bernie of voting against the auto bailout. It is not quite true, but it resonates in a state that Obama saved with the loans that also saved Wall Street. It seems easy to convince Michigan that Obama is still the man and that Bernie is to his left. However, Bernie's numbers continue to hold and rise in the crucial state.

Bernie stepped into a racial dispute during the debate. Addressing a Don Lemon question about James Comey's borrowed phrase while speaking about policing: "everyone is a little bit racist," Bernie Sanders said:

"When you are white, you don't know what it is like to be living in a ghetto, you don't know what it is like to be poor. You don't know what it's like to be hassled when you walk down the street or you get dragged out of a car."

Bernie does not truly deserve all the outrage and disgust that are following that remark today, Monday, March 7. Bernie is an old white Jew from Vermont, although he was born in New York. He uses terms he knows. Yes, "ghetto" may connote crime, poverty, and deprivation, but it is not a black thing. He should know the Jewish origin of the term in Venice, Italy. As in struggling to rise quickly from slipping down on an icy pitch, Bernie made the matter worse by commenting further today: "What I meant to say is when you talk about ghettos, traditionally what you are talking about is African-American communities."

This is not true, but the debate is another story for another day. It is unforgivable coming from a man of recent Jewish-Polish extraction. This sort of unforced error delights Hillary Clinton's camp; it keeps the votes of African Americans solidly in her column.

Senator Sanders is not the only one to misspeak. Former Secretary of State Madeleine Albright walked back her speech on women who do not support others: "I understand that I came across as condemning those who disagree with my political preferences." She had said in early February, before the New Hampshire State primaries that Hillary eventually lost as expected: "Just remember, there's a special place in hell for women who don't help each other."

Yesterday, Dr. Albright revisited the comment in Fox Business Network's program, *Mornings with Maria,* and spoke with the anchor Maria Bartiromo.

> "I have used that statement now for two decades; it even ended up on a Starbucks cup. I should not have used it in the context of voting, but I do think women should help each other. I think it is not that easy; I think we need to have a discussion about it, but I should have used it in that context."

The email scandal continues to trail Hillary. Her supporters do not seem to worry. She is old at the game, and her endurance for marathon campaigns knows no bounds, except against a certain Kenyan-American man named Barack, Barack Obama. Bernie is in for a long race that Hillary is destined to win. Once the winner-takes-all states roll in, the Democrats will close the book on Bernie and thank him for running and rustling the base. However, if the race gets any closer, bad blood may flow and affect Hillary in the general elections.

No matter who emerges as the Democratic Party nominee, history will record a first whenever Hillary or Bernie throws in the towel. Either the first woman nominee of a major American political party emerges, or the first Jew and self-styled socialist will take the banner of Democrats. Whoever triumphs, New York will get a lot of attention in the coming months: Trump, Hillary, and Bernie have roots in New York, so does the *real* billionaire of New York, NY Michael Bloomberg—though he was born in Brighton, Boston, MA.

6

Of Bloomberg and Carson

Exit without Entry

Also happening on Monday, March 7, 2016, ex-Mayor Michael Rubens Bloomberg quit what he never began: run for the presidency as a third-party candidate. He gave the same reason that Henry Ross Perrot had given in 1992: chances of pushing the election of the next president to the Congress. Mayor Bloomberg defined his running and triggering the possible election of Donald Trump or, worse, Ted Cruz as *"The risk I will not take"*:

> In a three-way race, it's unlikely any candidate would win a majority of electoral votes, and then the power to choose the president would be taken out of the hands of the American people and thrown to Congress. The fact is, even if I were to receive the most popular votes and the most electoral votes, victory would be highly unlikely, because most members of Congress would vote for their party's nominee. Party loyalists in Congress—not the American people or the Electoral College—would determine the next president. [7]

---

[7] http://www.bloombergview.com/articles/2016-03-07/the-2016-election-risk-that-michael-bloomberg-won-t-take

The Boston-born 74-year-old CEO of Bloomberg conglomerate spares us another New Yorker in a busy field of New Yorkers (Hillary, Sanders, and Trump), each with about seven decades of earthly existence. Curiously, Bloomberg is making a big deal of exiting from a race he never entered. There are far too many people eyeing the very big house at 1600 Pennsylvania Avenue, Washington, DC—the Obama White House. Unless one declares publicly for the presidency and makes some moves to campaign for votes, the normal thing to say is, 'I am not running.' Again, these are not normal times.

There are no reported negative reactions from either Trump or Hillary Clinton. The reactions are not as blooming as those that followed Vice President Joe Biden's withdrawal without wading into the campaign arena last October. Will Bloomberg also play a Perot and make an entry... reentry if things go way south for both parties? It is doubtful. Hillary Clinton and Donald Trump are set to emerge. It seems that Americans are set to change the Republican Party for good or to elect the first female president.

In quitting, Mike Bloomberg made a good call. The elections of 2016 will not be about money, or he would have stayed the course, as he did in New York City and won an unprecedented third term.

> Quitting is not giving up; it's choosing to focus your attention on something more important. Quitting is not losing confidence; it's realizing that there are more valuable ways you can spend your time.[8]

---

[8] Osayi Emokpae Lasisi, *Impossible is Stupid*

Medical Hero, Political Zero

Today, 3.7.16, Rachael Maddow's *TRMS* finally poofed Dr. Ben Carson off the 17 president-wannabe candidates who started the race to the White House on the Republican ticket. Carson ended his lackluster campaign to some scant oh-ing at the C-PAC convention last Friday. He claimed that many people love him, but they will not vote for him. Some love! Again, another African American makes the flash in GOP and pulverizes in the tradition of Alan Keyes and Herman "999" Cain. The African-American community lost a role model who just whitewashed his stellar successes and dirtied his "gifted hands" in the pigsty of politics.

From where does the Republican Party find men who speak as if some strange scientists brewed and bred them on another planet! My contention is that a focused and sensible African American can make the presidency through the party. Alas, the party has veered right to the deep end since General Colin Powell and Dr. Condoleezza Rice. The likes of Alan Lee Keyes and Benjamin Solomon "Ben" Carson, Sr. corrupt the core concept of conservatism with their nugatory narrow-mindedness. If President George W. Bush could be a 'compassionate conservative,' what reasons do these African-American politicians offer for sounding so outside the norm?

Dr. Carson is worthy of emulation. No one should say 'good riddance to bad rubbish'; however, it is a relief to see him leave the stage: Carson the politician has become an embarrassment to everything that the brilliant and excellent neurosurgeon achieved.

His peculiar nerdish calmness stands in stark contrast to the fire-eating rhetoric of Trump, the frontrunner. Mr. Trump has been stroking the flames of violence by inciting people to "knock the hell out of" protesters and promising to pay their legal bills. He knows too well that he will not pick up the legal cost of defending criminals from his campaign chest, especially-God forbid—murderers. Carson has seen the color of anger in his younger years, and he does not like it.

Trump stokes anger. He must learn to let go and sanitize his political rhetoric; or, as in all cases of vendors of prejudice and parochial populism, it will consume him. As a business executive, Trump should know when a brand is no longer selling, when to change course, and when to adopt winning strategies. Nothing marks Donald Trump as rabid Republican. Possibly, he is playing populist card to suck in the needed base that decides the primary elections. Thereafter, many of those who are currently in Trump train will hitch a ride home to where they belong—not in Trump's camp.

Of course, since success has many aunts and uncles, many more will hop on board for the continued ride. The latter passengers will come from his economic class and world of influence. Trump will not cater to the interest of all those who troop out to cheer him on in large theaters across the country—if he wins, which is likely. The American hunger for change after eight years of Obama is thick in the air. Either in Hillary or in Trump, Americans with get the change they seek.

We are watching; the whole world is watching.

7

Super Tuesday Reloaded

Presidential primaries are complicated; they call for closer studies. The two main parties have different numbers of delegates required to win the nomination, and they allocate different numbers to different states of the union, depending on the population and party members, I presume. Different states have different criteria for the allocation of state delegates to the national convention. Some are caucuses; other are primaries. Primaries are like regular elections; caucuses are village elections: one person, one vote at a set time, place, and date.

Today, March 8, is "Super Tuesday" reloaded, a smaller part-two version of last week's primary edition. Democrats in Michigan and in Mississippi voted, while Republicans in the following states also voted: Idaho, Hawaii, Michigan, and Mississippi. Hillary Clinton beat Bernie Sanders in Mississippi by a wide margin (29-4 delegates), thanks to older African Americans who are yet to buy into the socialist promises of Senator Sanders. Younger and more politically active Blacks, who did not experience the Clinton era, visibly support Sanders.

Speaking from nearby Cleveland, Ohio, Hillary harped on "results, not insults," "corporate patriotism," "breaking down barriers," "equal pay for equal work," "turning mourning into movement," and other vintage Clintonesque speak. There were slight interruptions from the audience, probably from haughty hecklers and or anti-Clinton activists. Television cameras did not show them. Calm restored.

Results from Michigan showed that, contrary to the polls, Bernie got a bigger chunk of the available 147 delegates (65-58). It was so unexpected that Sanders did not plan to address his supporters; he was already in Florida! The talking heads will have a great week analyzing how Sanders came from behind and snatched victory in Michigan of all places. The Democratic CNN-Facebook-Univision debate holds tomorrow. Although more issue-orientated than the GOP schoolyard brawl, it will add to this great upset. No one in Clinton's camp will miss the surprising primary results from Dearborn, Michigan; they are pregnant with possible problems.

Dearborn, a Detroit suburb, is home to many Arab Americans: Iraqi, Lebanese, Palestinians, Yemeni, etc. Bernie, the Jew, beats Hillary in Dearborn by, as Donald Trump will say, "a lot" (59–39%). Apparently, in the age of Obama, Americans are focusing on other factors beyond religion and ethnicity. The supposedly Muslim-hating Trump beat the still-crowded field of Republicans by a whopping 36% of the votes, while John Kasich from neighboring Ohio got 24%, as did Ted Cruz. Thus, in Michigan and with 12% margin of defeat, Kasich saw signs that the promised sweep of his home state of Ohio next week has a leg on the banana peel.

Trump continued the winning streak in the hunt for Republican delegates, making it more difficult to stop his outright victory. Speaking from Jupiter, Florida, Trump sounded humble, more conciliatory, but still boastful. He called Romney "a good man" and thanked Megyn Kelly for saying the truth about his winnings! The man has set his eyes in uniting the party as a "unifier" and a "commonsense conservative" and then taking on Hillary Clinton in the general elections. Cruz, Kasich, and Rubio now have to kneel down and endure some rounds of the rosary; they will need Hail Marys next week, March 15: Super Tuesday, part three. The trio must pray hard on their religious convictions, *push* —pray until something happens. At this point, only a divine intervention will see anyone but Trump through.

The camp of Ted Cruz played the Carson card again—as it had done in January Iowa Caucus. A report stated that a tweet from Cruz's Hawaii field office had asserted that Marco Rubio was dropping out of the race, that a vote for him would be a wasted vote. Cruz did not have to do the memo; Rubio has no way forward. He might as well quit after tonight's results.

The average Floridian knows that his or her vote for Senator Marco Rubio next week will change nothing. In a winner-takes-all situation, the stakes could not be higher. The only viable alternative to Trump is Senator Ted Cruz. Sadly, Cruz is not a choice that levelheaded Republicans want to consider for 2016. If Ted Cruz does not win Florida, he too should do what Jeb Bush has suggested jokingly: Drop his pants and moon the whole shebang. Cruz does not look like quitting; the thought of Trump beating him makes him very anxious.

TRUSTED

Calgary, Canada-born Cuban-American Senator Ted (Rafael Edward) Cruz (R-TX) came to Congress as a one-man demolition army. He is a filibuster maestro, an anti-Obama activist, and an enthusiastic evangelical. In 2013, he angered Nigerian Americans when he mocked the website debacle of Obamacare rollout. He told supporters in Houston, TX: "You may have noticed that all the Nigerian email scammers have become a lot less active lately; they all have been hired to run the Obamacare website." Houstonian Nigerians and the Christian Association of Nigerian-Americans (CANAN) did not find funny the "distasteful and disparaging" quip. Disappointed Nigerian Ambassador Ade Adefuye deplored the remark and demanded an apology.

Ironically, Nigerian Americans see Mrs. Heidi Suzanne Cruz as one of them: She accompanied her missionary dentist parents on trips to Nigeria and Obama's Kenya. Sadly, Senator Ted Cruz has not met a constituency he will not offend. There are inexplicable features about Cruz that make him easily unlikeable. Yet, to the natural dilemma, he adds avoidable and unstudied verbal diarrhea.

Today, besides getting the nod of Carly Fiorina, who had dropped off the race after New Hampshire, Cruz warmed up to the idea of a contested convention. He had called it "illegal and wrong." The convention seems to be the only wall of tungsten that could stop the Trump train. Ted Cruz's winnings do not impress the establishment, even as Rubio looks likely to fail and fall off in Florida. His only other hope at this point is that the party will find him more acceptable to Trump.

Like Michelle Obama, Ted Cruz is Princeton-Harvard educated. He is a bright lawyer who clerked for Supreme Court Chief Justice William Rehnquist, and he is a lively debater. His politics is another story. Ted Cruz misjudged Trump badly. He must blame himself for cuddling Trump, if he loses the primaries to Trump. The Ted Cruz campaign strategy was simple: He hoped to inherit Trump's supporters. For months, he gave nods to controversial statements by Trump, flashing a smirk when he should have frowned at the invectives. Cruz stood aloof as Trump's tongue-lashing drowned Jeb Bush. With Trump standing strong and bashing him too, Cruz saw the light before Damascus, and declared, "Trump has a tenuous relationship with the truth."

The mainstream media rarely check the facts and hardly hold Trump down to obvious untruths. His fast talks and surplus claims make it hard to pin him down. I have seen no resolute resolve to crosscheck Trump since Fox's Megyn Kelly tackled him. MSNBC's Joe Scarborough and Mika Brzezinski deliver such softballs you wonder whether Donald Trump owns the show. Last night, without any prompting, Trump pitched products that Romney had mentioned in his listing of Trump's failed businesses. He challenged the media to fact-check his claims about successful steak, wine, water, and glossy magazine businesses. It takes only a few clicks to prove otherwise. In fact, Trump himself disproved the claim about *Trump* magazine, which went out of circulation many moons ago: He showed *The Jewel of Palm Beach!* Trump may lend his name to products, fine; but to claim the products as 100% his own businesses was stretching the truth too thin.

Ted Cruz is right: Trump is very creative with the truth. He has a way of building his own facts with a small quantity of truth. Ted himself is not an evangelical angel; he finds it easy to call people liars. In July 2015, he accused Majority Leader Mitch McConnell (R-KY), of "a simple lie," and of "[willingness] to say things that he knows are false." Such brashness and rudeness have earned him no endorsement from his fellow senators. The party establishment does not trust Ted Cruz, even if a miracle happens and he is able to stop Trump. His only chance now is a rumble at the Cleveland, Ohio convention in July. On the flip-flop about contested convention, Trump is bound to pounce and continue to castigate Cruz as a liar with the "Lyin' Ted" epithet.

Lyin' Ted or *Little Marco*, no matter how anyone slices or dices the primaries, Republican stakeholders or the establishment entities are not a cheerful crowd. Their top contenders, Donald Trump and Ted Cruz, are like the two proverbial knives in a bachelor's pad: the sharp knife has no handle; the one with a handle is not sharp. In the end, Trump will trump Ted, and the good advice of Mama McCain will come in handy: The party will close its nose and take Trump.

The electoral system has tied the knots. The Republicans have taken delivery of a product they did not order. It is going to be a year to remember. Lose or win, the party is in for a rough ride pre- and post-2016. Win, Trump hijacks the party; lose, Trump redefines the Republican primaries. The influence of moneybags will diminish drastically. Just saying some outrageous stuff will bring the media to eat from a politician's palms and keep ratings off the scale.

8

Debates Unlimited

Last night, Wednesday, March 9, Mrs. Clinton and Sanders sucked airtime off CNN-Facebook-Univision sponsored tête-à-tête in Dade County, Florida. I was not expecting much, and not much happened. Jorge Ramos, the Univision anchor whom Trump threw out of his press conference last year, got the limelight by asking whether Hillary would step down if indicted. She was not prepared to glorify the hypothetical question with an answer, and she was right: indict her for what?

There are many debates, town hall meetings, and one-on-one interviews. The media wait to get a *gotcha* going… anything that will bring down a politician. They do not have to investigate: they sit back and listen. If everything fails, Trump fills the void. He delivers. You can take the theory to a bank teller and cash it, no signature required! Today, Thursday, March 10, 2016, Republicans featured again on CNN. The debate was more conciliatory—for Trump Ted Crux and Marco Rubio huffed and puffed; Kasich stayed true his self-characterization as "the adult in the house."

Trump failed to throw more red meat to his fans, who would take his words as gospel and act on them. During an event in North Carolina, a white man sucker-punched a BLM youth whom the police were escorting out of the venue. The youth ended up thrown to the ground and arrested! A video of the encounter led to an arrest of the elderly white dude for assault. No legal help came from Trump. In a chat with Anderson Cooper and as if to give his supporters something to chew as the debate tone softened, he offered: "Islam hates America." Such added fodder to the fire that Trump had lit make Republican debates notorious. Much more than virtue, notoriety sells like sex.

The debate in Miami, FL was policy-driven with fewer polemics. True to type, Trump branded the Democratic debates as being a "very, very boring thing to watch"! Some issues addressed were interesting to those who had not tuned off from the playground parleys that CNN was serving. The detour from the new norm was dramatic. Trump rose to the status of a serious candidate with few specifics, such as leaving Social Security as-is and knocking "the hell out of" ISIS. Everything else is negotiable: making better deals with China, Cuba, Japan, Iran, Mexico, etc.

Trump opened up on his family tree. As if to erase the booing of his pro-Israel claim, he offered, "I have tremendous love for Israel. I happen to have a son-in-law and a daughter that are Jewish, Okay? And two grandchildren that are Jewish." I doubt the revelation will sit well with his white supremacist supporters, who are both racist and anti-Semitic. Then again, Trump is almost way beyond their reproach at this point.

Next week's primaries will reveal whether the new and improved Trump sells better than the older version. Like all new products, some people will take a second look and or adopt a wait-and-see neutrality. One thing is certain, if Trump beats Rubio "by a lot" or not in winner-takes-all Florida, Marco will become another victim of Trump's Jinx: attack him personally (as he does to others) and you can sing solemnly your political Nunc Dimittis.

Meanwhile, today, Dr. Ben Carson let out that he will endorse Trump, who had likened Carson's self-described "pathological temper" to child molesting, for which, according to Donald Trump, "there is no cure." In an interview last November with CNN's *OutFront* with Erin Burnett: Trump offered:

> "It's in the book[9] that he's got a pathological temper. That's a big problem because you don't cure that ... as an example: child molesting. You don't cure these people. You don't cure a child molester. There's no cure for it. Pathological, there's no cure for that."

In leaning to endorse Trump, Dr. Carson implied that Trump has a bipolar persona. It is a bit surprising that people are now diagnosing one another of one chronic disease or the other. He told Fox News:

> "There's two Donald Trumps. There's the Donald Trump that you see on television and who gets out in front of big audiences, and there's the Donald Trump behind the scenes. They're not the same person. One's very much an entertainer, and one is actually a thinking individual."

---

[9] Gifted Hands: The Ben Carson Story by Ben Carson, MD with Cecil Murphy

American politics is magical. The primaries tow the same trajectory of *American abracadabra*, as we called all magical acts in teenage years too long gone. How else do we explain that after the badmouthing and bad behaviors, the participants in the verbal war of political pugilists take chill pills and work together for the good of the country? I still recall then Senator Joe Biden patronizing then Senator Obama in the 2008 Democratic primaries. By the end of 2015, now Vice President Joe Biden had become a big brother to now President Barack Obama. Mrs. Clinton's "Shame on you, Barack Obama," resonated for many moons. Barack Obama is now her greatest supporter in the background (or Joe Biden would have stepped up—as urged by his late son, Beau).

Now, Dr. Carson is poised to endorse a man who has compared him to a child molester, a felon. This too is sheer magic. More magical is that Trump explained it away as mere fighting words in trying to overcome an opponent in tough election primaries. To Trump, it is as if he is a participant in a real-life *Apprentice,* show, where the contestants beat down each other with words: the more caustic the words, the higher the score.

9

A Wacky Weekend

On Friday, March 11, Dr. Ben Carson followed the footsteps of Christie and endorsed Trump. Thus, Carson kicked up some dust in what I had expected to be a fairly calmer weekend. It started with the burial of former First Lady Nancy Reagan. I planned to catch up with the visit of Canadian Prime Minister Justin Trudeau to the White House. Video clips showed Obama denying he had anything to do with the making of Trump and passing the ball back to Republicans, who watched as Trump made mock mountains out of Obama's birthplace. Obama touted the greatness of America, where a kid from Calgary, Canada could run for the presidency of USA: a swipe at Ted Cruz. Obama was making fun and enjoying it.

My plan turned to daydreaming after I got home; the primary elections took turns never before seen in modern times. The Trump train ran into a solid wall in Chicago. The goading and calls for physical clashes got an answer in downtown Chicago. The main question is: Why did Trump campaign choose such a location at this point in his caustic campaign?

If the campaign team did not anticipate a protest, Trump should fire someone; if the team did anticipate trouble, then they got their money's worth: the clash of protesters pushed other presidential contenders out of Friday news coverage. The media, as is now the norm, fell for it. Trump won again; the news was all about him. The disrupted Chicago event buried both Bernie and Hillary at the tail end of newscasts. Whatever other candidates did, wherever they were, the media did not seem to care. Trump stayed above the fray and sounded like he was the Dalai Lama: "I don't want to see people hurt." This was coming from a man who preached the punching of people in the face and taking them out in stretchers. The development is troubling. Ironically, Bernie's polite handling of BLM activists last year now looks more rewarding than Trump's braggadocio.

Poor Marco Rubio! His call for supporters to vote for Kasich in Ohio next week, possibly with an eye on Kasich reciprocating, is now mute; ditto, his win in inconsequential DC caucus. Ted Cruz deftly stepped up to the mic and called for civility in the process. He offloaded on Trump's team for sowing the seeds of violence and asking for pledges to Trump! He is right. The man who sows storms will one day reap tsunami. Cruz did not forget to blame it on President Obama—just as other Republicans lately blame the President for everything socioeconomic, political, and cultural! Still, the media will not leave alone the protests at Trump rallies. An odd expectation that something will happen hangs in the air. The needless dredging up of Chicago 1968 in the Democratic Convention and the RFK assassination were eerie. We pray none repeats. *Oremus!*

Trump was on the campaign trail in Dayton, OH. In a hangar by his private plane, he went back to what he does best: entertain. Dr. Carson was right: Trump is an entertainer. He reads his audience, and he feeds folks with hackneyed phrases and many bloated half-truths. Between lampooning "Little Marco" and "Lyin' Ted," he fed jingoistic jingles to the crowd, not forgetting to blame Obama for everything he could recall. If anyone thought Trump was backing off, a test soon opened up: a group of protesters showed up. Hear Trump: "Just throw them the hell out." Trump did not spare Kasich on Leyman Brothers and on NAFTA, even making fun of him with "Kaysick"!

After he was done with his usual call for "taking back our country" and "making America great again," he turned to accusing Senator Sanders ("Bernie, our communist friend") of sponsoring the "troublemakers," "thugs," and "wise guys." As Trump enjoyed the name-calling, Security Service agents jumped up the stage to protect Trump from some fellow who suddenly rushed forward on live television and bull-charged the podium. The police arrested a 32-year-old man and charged him with "inducing panic and disorderly misconduct."

Trump swung through Cleveland, OH. Before he got to Kansas City, MO, the protesters had devised a strategy that successfully disrupted Trump's rally a bit. Trump told that they were Bernie Sanders' supporters, that Moveon.org supported them, and that they were "so bad for our country." In the same breath as he asked the police to "get them out of here," he said, "We don't want to hurt the protesters; we love our protesters"!

Why?

Trump believes the presence of protesters forces the media to turn their cameras to show the size of his rallies! He lambastes the media as the "worst people," yet he knows the cameras will stay there to broadcast every word. Trump has mastered "the art of the deal" in milking media time without paying a dime!

The violence in Vandalia, OH rattled Trump, obviously. He lived the 1960s. On CNN, the campaign of 1968 screened in *The Sixties*, a documentary. On June 6, 1968, Sirhan Sirhan shot and killed the 42-year-old Democratic presidential candidate, Senator Robert F. Kennedy. He never made it to the Convention in Chicago, where bloody violence later erupted—as it did yesterday. Earlier that year on April 4, the same RFK had announced to his supporters the assassination of Dr. Martin Luther King, Jr. in Memphis, Tennessee.

As in 1968, the whole world was watching!

Today marks the first time anyone came close to attacking Trump physically. He must know that it could have been worse, that some nut could do him harm. In 2016, it is harder to wreck such a havoc, but there are more mentally loose nuts in America than metallic nuts in a junkyard. Add the present terrorism dimension and the fear becomes real. Trump mouthed that the attack on him was, maybe, ISIS-related! He was exaggerating, of course. He stated that it was wrong for the judge to let his attacker out on bail. He vowed to start pressing charges against protesters. Trump is on every television channels, even on C-SPAN. Carson got it right again: Trump is an entertainer and, indeed, a thinking man; but, more troubling, if the pundits and former associates are right, he may be dangerous too.

10

The Eve of Elimination

It is Pi-Day, 3.14.2106. The campaigning heat is on—on the Republican Party primaries and caucuses. The Democrats are on a long haul, no matter the outcome of another so-called "Super Tuesday." Democrats have no winner-takes-all contests, so the haunt and harvest of delegates will drag on for more months. The Republicans have bigger goats to roast. The party elders have realized that Rubio is cooked and settled on John Kasich. Trump and Ted Cruz remain unacceptable to them, for now.

Former Speaker John Boehner has endorsed John Kasich, and Mitt Romney is campaigning for him. Kasich hangs his hats on Ohio, make or break. He is haughty about it: The governor refuses to reciprocate Senator Rubio's support in Ohio. Kasich's campaign lets out that it will succeed in Ohio on its own and Rubio should fall on his sharp sword in Florida all by himself!

Ohio lives up to its tested tradition of deciding Republican primaries, as I glean from the ongoing CNN documentary, *Road for the White House.* In 1860, Abe Lincoln had no path to becoming the party's nominee.

His façade of an honest politician prevented him from succumbing to dirty tricks directly, but he had a clever campaign manager. Ohio switched its votes from Senator William Henry Seward (R-NY) to Lincoln. Pennsylvania delivered the last straw. Lincoln went on to become a consequential president in the history of America. Is history set to repeat itself? A few more hours will tell.

Trumpmania continues. The media catch up on Trump's truthlessness, which he delivers "sufficiently sugared." On NBC's *Meet The Press* yesterday, Chuck Todd challenged the Trump-alleged ISIS connection of the man who had jumped onto his stage. Trump did not back down. Today, in an interview with Chris Christie sitting in, Trump called the protests "a lovefest" that helps his campaign!

DECISION DAY

The Ides of March has come. The Republican race to the White House must tighten today. For Democrats, Bernie may pull off some surprises as in Michigan, but it will not dent Hillary much; she is set to win: Bernie is no Barack. This is 2016—not 2008! The Republicans may present some drama as the primaries go provincial, if not native, but Rubio will be on his way out, win or lose. All eyes are on Kasich: If he loses his home state of Ohio to Mr. Trump, and Trump takes Florida from the homeboy (Rubio), then the game is over. Trump wins. Further attempts to muscle him out will decimate the Republican Party, as happened to the Democratic Party in 1968. The story of what happens today will shape the politics of these United States beyond the year 2020.

The results are trickling in, and there are no surprises. Rubio loses his home state of Florida to a part-time-resident and business mogul from New York. As expected, he throws in the towel. To his great relief, Kasich wins his home state of Ohio. He announces that he is going to Philadelphia. Is he following the path of Lincoln? He is already touting the phrase: "As Ohio goes, so goes the nation." Kasich lives to fight again.

Trump won in Florida, North Carolina, Illinois, and, earlier, he had picked up nine delegates from the Commonwealth of the Northern Mariana Islands. With all his wins so far, he is not halfway to clinching the nomination. He returns to his palatial Palm Beach, FL estate for the usual stream-of-the-conscience speech that touches on everything old and new, from the unending announcements of Ivanka giving birth to her child any second to weird respects for Todd Palin, Sarah Palin's husband who has had another snowmobile accident. Trump's speeches are becoming so predictable they no longer excite. The gallery of generalities will not fly in *normal* general elections, but these are not normal times.

Trump has mastered the art of political publicity. As Hitler's Nazi Joseph Goebbels posited, "If you tell a lie big enough and keep repeating it, people will eventually come to believe it." Lies do have short legs, but far too many short legs can complete the race of a lone long-legged truth, albeit for a short period in the history of humans. Tonight, MSNBC's Brian Williams and Rachael Maddow did not cringe when Donald Trump pointed out reporters covering his speech and called them, "disgusting."

A new normal!

The media normalize Trump at every turn. These same topnotch newspersons of supposedly Democratic bent ignored Bernie Sanders' speech tonight at an event somewhere in the country while waiting for Trump to exhale! I could not believe what is unfolding before my eyes. In some climes, one would say that Mr. Trump has cast a juju spell on the media. They seem to worship his image, and he is still among the living!

I wonder if anyone has checked on our Ted Cruz today. It is sad. To far too many in the media, Trump is an entertainer, a sort of "serious comedian" running for the highest office of the land. I am not surprised. I am not worried: I have lived in America long enough to know that the news media will take all the bullcrap as the balloon inflates and delight in watching it deflate. They make and break. They media never fail.

Earlier today, Trump expressed delight with his campaign manager Corey R. Lewandowski. In an op-ed in *The Washington Times*, Thursday, March 10, a female reporter with the conservative news site *Breitbart*, Ms. Michelle Fields, alleged that Lewandowski grabbed her by the arm during the press conference of Tuesday night in Jupiter, Florida. Trump's campaign denied the incident.

Ms. Fields tweeted a photo of her bruised arm to Lewandowsky and Trump: "I guess these just magically appeared on me. So weird." The news site did not stand by her. Hence, she and a colleague quit *Breitbart News*. Unbeknownst to many, Steve (Stephen Kevin) Bannon, the executive chair of *Breitbart,* is a staunch supporter of Trump. Justice, if any for Ms. Fields, could only come from the local law enforcement.

11

Marco Rubio Voted Out

My colleagues who support Trump are quick to give him a pass on his verbal diarrhea: *That's the way he talks, but he speaks the truth.* The claim is contestable. Truth has no shades. There are only three sides to every contention, especially in matrimony: his side, her side, and the facts. Facts are sacred; there are no versions. One of my female colleagues told me at lunch last Friday that Rubio lost his mind by referring to the color of Trump's hair and alluding to the size of his penis, that it showed Rubio was not ready for prime time, and that he had more growing to do. I doubt she was alluding to the 25-year gap between Trump and Rubio.

Who is Rubio?

Marco Antonio Rubio is a 45-year-old Cuban-American politician, a lawyer by profession, and an adjunct professor. He was the Speaker of Florida House of Representatives before becoming a US senator from Florida. Rubio emerged on the national stage when the Republicans nominated him to respond to President Obama's state of the union address in 2013.

Senator Rubio looked nervous enough for such a primetime show; then he took a quick water break in the middle of the speech—and the cameras were rolling! Just as I had told a friend that Barack Obama was a president-in-waiting after the 2004 Boston convention speech, I told the same friend (a Republican) that Marco just blew the bridge to the next stage.

The water-break incident did not quite disrupt his path to the presidency, though Trump dramatized it on a few odd occasions while belittling "Little Marco." In a normal election cycle, Rubio would have gone far. If all failed, he could land a vice presidential position, for which Mitt Romney considered him in the 2012 race. Rubio's rapid rise left the depth of his Senate records unexplored. They show in the immigration bill he has abandoned, and they show in the almost mechanical regurgitation of his otherwise impressive oratory. Simply stated, Marco Rubio has little depth in these primary elections.

Senator Marco Rubio went very low on Trump, mocking his spray-tan complexion and alluding that he (Trump) wet his pants during a debate. Rubio does not have the maturity of Kasich; he is only 45. He does not have the rooted pedigree of Jeb Bush, his mentor; he is a first-generation American, the son of Cuban immigrants with fourth-grade education—or so he claims. Rubio told *Fox and Friends* in July 2015 that he would bring back "a level of class" to the White House.

> "We already have a president now that has no class. I mean, we have a president now that, you know, does selfie stick videos, that invites YouTube stars there, people that, you know, eat cereal out of a bathtub."

How does Rubio compare himself with Obama, a president of Harvard law review, whose university-graduate parents were light years ahead of their peers? When Rubio got the chance to display the "level of class" that his fourth-grade, bartender father bestowed on him, he stepped into the deep end of a puerile penile political pigsty. It is no wonder Trump's supporters accept low blows from Trump: he does not claim to be political royalty; Rubio does. Class indeed! Rubio is a hypocrite. He wants to keep out of USA all uneducated immigrants, when his own parents came with fourth-grade education and spoke only Spanish. His bill might have kept out the biological father of Steve Jobs!

Rubio is out. He lost very badly to Mr. Trump. He won just one county out of the 67 counties. The good people of Florida apparently disapproved of his job in the Senate and his politics: his refusal to listen and yield to former Governor Jeb Bush and the way he ran his campaign lately like a leaky-mouth lout. Good riddance to pretense, to hypocrisy, to flip-flops on immigration, and to the pleasing of radical Tea Party. Both Cruz and Kasich applauded Rubio. Trump gave him great kudos: "He's tough, he's smart, and he's got a great future." One may agree, but Rubio still has a lot more to learn.

I saw the future of Republican Party I like during the South Carolina primaries. Rubio pointed out nicely the prominent supporters standing on the podium with him: Governor Nikki Haley, an Indian American, Senator Tim Scott, an African American, U.S. Rep. Trey Gowdy, a European American, and himself, a Cuban American. This is what Mrs. Haley had referred to as "Benetton commercial"—a unity of colors in the party.

Senator Rubio's parting speech sounded as if he wrote it for the acceptance speech at the firmly foreseen "Chaos in Cleveland" Convention and later recast it to reflect the unfolding reality. A part of the speech reminds me of Barack Obama's 2004 speech in Boston, Massachusetts. Unfortunately, Rubio's delivery of 2016 is poor in comparison with Obama 2004, but the words are memorable:

> I ask the American people: Do not give in to the fear. Do not give in to the frustration. We can disagree about public policy, we can disagree about it vibrantly, passionately. But we are a hopeful people, and we have every right to be hopeful. For we in this nation are the descendants of go-getters. In our veins runs the blood of people who gave it all up so we would have the chances they never did. We are all the descendants of someone who made our future the purpose of their lives. We are the descendants of pilgrims. We are the descendants of settlers. We are the descendants of men and women that headed westward in the Great Plains not knowing what awaited them. We are the descendants of slaves who overcame that horrible institution to stake their claim in the American Dream. We are the descendants of immigrants and exiles who knew and believed that they were destined for more, and that there was only one place on earth where that was possible. This is who we are, and let us fight to ensure that this is who we remain. For if we lose that about our country, we will still be rich and we will still be powerful, but we will no longer be special.

Beauty-full!

12

Supreme Scuffle

Barack Obama dared the Republican-controlled Senate this sunrise, Wednesday, March 16, 2016. The day after the third "Super Tuesday" in March, the president announced that he had chosen Judge Merrick Garland, chief justice for the U.S. Court of Appeals for DC Circuit, as his Supreme Court (SCOTUS) nominee. If confirmed by the Senate, the respected jurist will occupy the seat left open by the death of Justice Antonin Scalia. I told colleagues that Obama would pick neither a woman (after Sonia Sotomayor and Elena Kagan—unless Ruth Ginsberg retires) nor a minority. That would be kicking the wall with two feet, fighting many battles on one warfront.

The nomination of a Supreme Court justice is a big event in modern American society. It is a powerful and independent institution, free from the interference of both the executive and the Congress. The Supreme Court can overrule both branches of government as well as the lower courts. It is a lifetime appointment. The nine members are the law lords; anything they agree on is the final say of the Constitution.

At first, it seemed like the news had sucked the air out of discussions about a potential Clinton-Trump face-off in November. The argument of the Republicans is for Obama not to nominate anyone for SCOTUS now. This is similar to telling the President to stop work! The constitution mandates President Obama to do exactly what he has done. Not to consider a nominee is shirking Senate's duty, which is what Senate Republicans have been doing to slow down the wheel of justice under President Obama. This sort of street strategy helps to breed the likes of Donald J. Trump.

By all published accounts, the Illinois-born and Harvard Law-graduate Garland, 63, is "a serious man and exemplary judge." Obama chose him from a slate of top contenders, including Sri Srinivasan (a judge in the same circuit as Garland), and Paul Watford, a judge in the 9th Circuit in San Francisco, CA. Judge Srinivasan would have presented added difficulties as the first Asian American to aspire to sit in the Supreme Court of the United States (SCOTUS).

Senate Majority Leader Addison Mitchell (Mitch) McConnell shot back immediately with what he termed "Biden Rule" of 1992, as if it backed the Republican antagonistic stand against any nominee of the president in an election year, no matter the qualification. "Biden Rule" does not exist, just a 1992 personal proposal of then Senator Joseph Robinette (Joe) Biden, Jr. The speech of Senator Joe Biden (D-DE) in June 1992 is still available on C-SPAN. Senator Mitch McConnell (R-KY) is a veteran political strategist. He knows of no such rule; he is just using any available argument to block another lifetime appointment by Obama.

Senator Mitch McConnell is wrong, obviously. Nothing logical supports the Republican position. He is merely using the Biden's opinion when he was a senator to obfuscate. President Obama has 300-plus days of his tenure. The Senate should do its job and not ride a phantom tiger. McConnell has dug in: "We've already made it very clear that a nomination for the Supreme Court by this President will not be filled this year," no matter who wins in the November elections. He might as well use "ever"—not "this year"— a hint of the level of hate McConnell harbors for Obama. Hear him:

> The next Supreme Court justice could fundamentally alter the direction of the court and our country for a generation, and the American people deserve a voice in such a momentous decision. This fair and reasonable approach is what Senate Judiciary Committee Chairman Chuck Grassley and I announced weeks ago and reiterated personally to the president.
>
> Our determination to allow the American people to have a voice has always been about a principle, not a person. It's called the "Biden Rule." As Vice President Biden said when he was Senate Judiciary Committee chairman, "Once the political season is under way, and it is, action on a Supreme Court nomination must be put off until after the election campaign is over." That, he said, "is what is fair to the nominee and is central to the process."

What other popular *voice* does the Senator from Kentucky want to hear? Unless he wants elected judges, the people have already spoken. Twice! They elected and reelected Barack Obama to the presidency. Are the Republicans waiting for Trump who is preaching lawlessness and promising riots to appoint a better judge? Alas, this is the way of politics. Let it play on!

Senator McConnell cares not about principles, nor about politics; he *cares* about a person: Obama. That Obama won a second term still troubles him. He needs to get one back to die happy. If this is it, so be it. This must rank as one of his happy moments, his only happy moment in eight years of Obama presidency.

Whether the Senate ever confirms Garland, or not, Obama has made his case. In doing so, he carves on marble the requirements of a Supreme Court justice:

> First, a justice should possess an independent mind, unimpeachable credentials, and an unquestionable mastery of law. There is no doubt this person will face complex legal questions, so it is imperative that he or she possess a rigorous intellect that will help provide clear answers.

Donald Trump will not let Obama upstage his domination of the news. He rolls out missiles and fires them. First, he initiates an anti-Clinton campaign—as if he is already the nominee. Two, he balks at the prospect of another debate and buries it with a definite *nyet*. Trump's decision is correct: The debates are now far too many, and they are becoming boring and unproductive. Third, Trump takes up Ted Cruz's projection that a contested convention "would be an absolute disaster. I think the people would quite rightly revolt." Trump goes on further and tells CNN, "Bad things would happen. I think you'd have riots. I think you'd have riots. I'm representing a tremendous many, many millions of people."

The Republican Party has a big battle on its hands. The elephant in the china shop is their creation: Trump.

13

Lindsey Graham Picks Poison

St. Patrick's Day, Thursday, March 15, third-term Republican Party Senator Lindsey Olin Graham, (senior senator from South Carolina) turned apparent absurdity upside down: he endorsed the presidential candidacy of fellow Senator Ted Cruz. When he threw his hat into the ring last year, I agreed with friends that he was not going to go too far. Senator John McCain, his friend, seemed to agree that it was a doomed project.

Senator Graham is a jolly-good fellow, but he has garnered neither the chutzpah nor the gravitas for such a high office as the presidency of USA. He is probably the highest unmarried political office holder in America. Cory Anthony Booker (D-NJ) and Timothy Eugene "Tim" Scott (R-SC), the only two African-American US senators, are also single. Graham is a first-generation graduate. He joined the Reserve Officers' Training Corps in college and has a bachelor's degree in psychology from the University of South Carolina in 1977. He graduated with a Juris Doctor from the same university in 1981.

Commissioned as an officer and Judge Advocate in the United States Air Force, he rose to the rank of colonel. He joined the South Carolina Air National Guard and the U. S. Air Force Reserve. He served in the South Carolina House of Representatives, United States House of Representatives and, in 2002, he ran for and won the seat formally occupied by controversial Senator James Strom Thurmond, who served in the Senate for 48 years.

In June 2015, Graham announced his candidacy. Introduced by his sister Darline Graham Nordone, Graham announced his candidacy for President. It was a lackluster campaign. His effort got no traction worth remembering, except that he called Trump a "jackass" on CNN. Trump returned fire. His falling campaign ran into a ditch. He tried to crawl out by making light of his cell phone number that Trump had shared on air. He never made it to the main debate lineup; he stayed in the hardly watched, so-called 'kids' table' with the likes of Bobby Jindal, George Pataki, and Rick Santorum.

Six months later, on December 21, 2015, Graham suspended his campaign for the presidency. He first endorsed Jeb Bush, going against the state political leaders [Governor Nikki Nimrata Haley, Senator Timothy Eugene "Tim" Scott, and Congressman Harold Watson "Trey" Gowdy) who went for Senator Marco Rubio. Both Bush and Rubio fell off the presidential podium: Jeb Bush quit after Super Tuesday loss in South Carolina, and Marco Rubio gave up the campaign ghost after the third Super Tuesday flop in his home state of Florida. At that point, it became obvious that there was no avoiding Mr. Donald J. Trump.

The conjecture about America electing a bachelor president rested with Mr. Graham's exit. Two American presidents came to the White House as bachelors. James Buchanan served a term (1857-1861) and never married. The great Abraham Lincoln succeeded in 1861. In 1885, another bachelor made it: From Caldwell, NJ, Stephen Grover Cleveland won as a bachelor; but, the next year in 1886, he married Frances Folsom (a woman under his avuncular and legal care and 28 years younger). It is worth noting that Mrs. Frances Cleveland was the first and only First Lady to marry in the White House.

Not only has he never married, Senator Graham apparently does not do emails. In March 2015, he told Chuck Todd in a *Meet The Press* interview that he had never sent an email! He is devoted to his sister, and I have heard him talk about a nephew. He sure looks like a good uncle and sounds like one. He flashes the smirk of a comedian that makes it easy to absorb some of his scorching speeches in describing fellow politicians.

On leaving the campaign trail, Graham did not let go of his criticisms of Trump and Cruz. He told CNN on January 21, "If you nominate Trump and Cruz, I think you get the same outcome. Whether it is death by being shot or poisoning, doesn't really matter. I don't think the outcome will be substantially different." On February 4, he rephrased the sentiment: "If you are a Republican and your choice is Donald Trump and Ted Cruz in a general election, it's the difference between poisoned or shot—you are still dead." Then he added, "On the question of foreign policy, the Texas senator is just as wrong as Obama, if not worse."

Three weeks later, on February 26, Graham expressed with morbid metaphor the level of hatred harbored by fellow senators towards Ted Cruz: "If you killed Ted Cruz on the floor of the Senate, and the trial was in the Senate, nobody would convict you." As if to lighten the tasteless joke, he said on the same day, "I was asked the hardest question in my political life: Do you agree with Donald Trump that Ted Cruz is the biggest liar in politics? Too close to call."

Yet, on Monday, March 21, 2016, Senator Graham will host a fundraising dinner for a man he has called an "opportunist": Senator Ted Cruz (R-TX).

Senator Graham did not hide his rejection of the remaining candidates: Donald Trump and Ted Cruz. With any one of them in the November elections, he believes the GOP will lose: "[I]t's the difference between poisoned or shot—you are still dead." Let us go with the poison-or-shot metaphor and assume that Senator Graham has aptly chosen shooting for Senator Ted Cruz, who loves to eat roast beef off the hot barrel of a fired and still smoking machine gun. This then leaves poison for Donald Trump.

If Trump were into literature, he would have provided the perfect retort:

> *"All right. Where is the poison? The battle of wits has begun. It ends when you decide and we both drink, and find out who is right... and who is dead."*[10]

---

[10] Man in Black, *The Princess Bride* (1987)

14

Mitt Meets Megyn

id-March, the Ides of March, is come and gone, and Trumps looks set to snatch the Republican Party nomination. If it happens, the party must hold its nose and bow to the will of "we the people." However, a month is a long time in politics. The only one person stumping Trump at this point is Trump himself. What worked at the beginning of a long race does not always work along the route. Most runners switch strategies, especially in marathons. They conserve energy at some points and accelerate as opponents creep up. Trump is far ahead of the game, and he is swaggering all over the track.

On Friday, March 18, Mitt Romney revs his anti-Trump drive. The ex-governor of Massachusetts, whose father George Romney was once governor of Michigan, surfaces in Utah, where he maintains a home in the Mormon homeland. In a surprising but tactical move, he sides with Ted Cruz in Utah caucuses, just days after campaigning with John Kasich to win Ohio. His reason: anything to stop Trump. Why? The following is from his Romney's Facebook wall:

> This week, in the Utah nominating caucus, I will vote for Senator Ted Cruz.
>
> Today, there is a contest between Trumpism and Republicanism. Through the calculated statements of its leader, Trumpism has become associated with racism, misogyny, bigotry, xenophobia, vulgarity and, most recently, threats and violence. I am repulsed by each and every one of these.
>
> The only path that remains to nominate a Republican rather than Mr. Trump is to have an open convention.

After his usual name-calling and tantrums aimed at Romney, Trump tweeted a piece that supported Mitt Romney's accusations of misogyny and vulgarity:

> Everybody should boycott the @megynkelly show. Never worth watching. Always a hit on Trump! She is sick, & the most overrated person on tv.[11]

Fox News will take it no more from the man it helped to create, a political novice that the talking heads at Fox packaged and presented to the public. For most of the Obama years, the Fox news channel that is the darling of conservatives demonized Barack Obama and Hillary Clinton nonstop. The network nurtured Donald Trump and a swarm of Tommy Tawms, the eventual electoral field troops of Mr. Trump.

Through a spokesperson, a certain Irena Briganti, the Fox News management fired back:

> "Donald Trump's vitriolic attacks against Megyn Kelly and his extreme, sick obsession with her is beneath the dignity of a presidential candidate who wants to occupy

---

[11] —Donald J. Trump (@realDonaldTrump) March 18, 2016

the highest office in the land. Megyn is an exemplary journalist and one of the leading anchors in America — we're extremely proud of her phenomenal work and continue to fully support her throughout every day of Trump's endless barrage of crude and sexist verbal assaults. As the mother of three young children, with a successful law career and the second highest rated show in cable news, it's especially deplorable for her to be repeatedly abused just for doing her job."

Trump's unnecessary consternation with the host of *The Kelly File* has dragged on for far too long. Since the first Fox News Republican Party primary debate last August, Trump has stayed on Ms. Megyn Kelly like an armor-plated head louse. He boycotted the second debate on Fox News because she was a moderator. Some pundits attribute his loss of Iowa caucus to his shunning of that debate and opening the door for Cruz to triumph. Trump relented during the third debate. He recently gave Megyn a shoutout after winning *bigly* on the second Super Tuesday. As with the "short-fingered vulgarian" remark, which Rubio has worsened and for which Trump often flashes his hands, Trump is a good giver of insults but a bad taker of subtle low blows.

One must wonder what Megyn Kelly said to get under Trump's trunks? On August 6, 2015, during the first debate on Fox News, Ms. Kelly asked a barrage of questions right off the bat. Her barbed statements really ruffled the feathers of an unprepared Mr. Trump. She challenged him on his derogatory sexist remarks. Here is the beginning of her litany of Trump's sexist remarks:

> Mr. Trump, one of the things people love about you is you speak your mind and you don't use a politician's filter. However, that is not without its downsides, in particular when it comes to women. You've called women you don't like fat pigs, dogs, slobs, and disgusting animals. Your twitter account--

True to his filter-free speak, Trump interjected with a lighthearted but indicting remark, "Only Rosie O'Donnell." His infamous gutter sniping with Ms. Rosie O'Donnell, then co-hosting Barbara Walter's *The View*, was the stuff for sleazy tabloids. Trump sounded funny and lowered the temperature a bit, but Ms. Kelly was not laughing. She pressed that the comments went beyond the scandalous exchanges with Ms. O'Donnell, to which Trump sarcastically agreed, "I'm sure it was."

Ms. Kelly was not done. She probably predicted Trump's interjection, but it only gave the audience time to recall and to anticipate her next move eagerly. In my mind, nothing more could be as climatic as what she had said, but her demeanor indicated that she was yet to land. She had not.

After what seemed like a grand gestation of grief, Megyn Kelly continued:

> Your Twitter account has several disparaging comments about women's looks. You once told a contestant that it would be a pretty picture to see her on her knees. Does that sound like the temperament of a man we should elect as president? And how do you answer the charge from Hillary Clinton, who is likely to be the Democratic nominee, that you are part of the war on women?

The contortion on Trump's forehead would have zapped a zika-infected Aedes mosquito to the hell of foolish flying pests. I doubt any fly would have been foolish enough to perch on his face there and then. Trump went off the tangent, driveling all over the place, and sounding rattled:

> The big problem this country has is being politically correct. I've been challenged by so many people, and I don't frankly have time for total political correctness. And to be honest with you, this country doesn't have time either. This country is in big trouble. We don't win anymore. We lose to China, we lose to Mexico both in trade and at the border. We lose to everybody. Frankly, what I say and oftentimes it's fun; it's kidding; we have a good time. What I say is what I say. And, honestly, Megyn if you don't like it, I'm sorry. I've been very nice to you, although I could probably not be based on the way you have treated me, but I wouldn't do that. But you know what? We, we need strength; we need energy; we need quickness; and we need brain in this country to turn it around. That I can tell you right now.

Many politicians would have let go, especially when and where some sympathized with Trump for being blindsided by such a perturbing poster of his unscrupulous utterances from another life. Trump refused to back down. As usual, he took to Twitter and talked about Megyn Kelly to whomever will listen. By 8.8.15, Trump dropped a sad and sexist shell in a CNN interview: He did not only degrade Ms. Kelly as "a lightweight," he offered graphically that she was angry: "You could see there was blood coming out of her eyes. Blood coming out of her wherever."

Trump lit up an inferno that could have derailed any mere-mortal politician. He beat the political storm by insisting that only sick minds thought he had meant Megyn was menstruating. He went on to say that he did not recognize sexism in the expression. He would also have someone find out where Megyn got the statements attributed to him. Maybe he will send investigators, like the one he allegedly sent to Hawaii to fish out Obama's birth certificate in 2011. We are still waiting for "what they're finding" that "they cannot believe"!

Just for the records, in a *Today Show* interview on NBC, April 7, 2011, Donald Trump insisted that his investigators were in Hawaii hunting for Obama's birth certificate.[12] Pressed by Meredith Vieira if he really had "people now out there searching—I mean, in Hawaii" searching for information he should know to be true. Trump retorted, "Absolutely. And they cannot believe what they're finding. And I'm serious—"

Curiously, no candidate brings the birther bait to the fore. It was a classic case of social lynching. Trump crossed all lines in a bid to demean Obama, just so he could clear the path to a Republican nomination in 2012. Republicans are not talking about it because they are guilty of complicity by their silence. Ted Cruz is the least credible voice in this case: he was actually born in Canada! Martin Niemöller, the anti-Nazi Protestant pastor would have told Ted, *"When they came for Obama, you remained silent... you were not Kenyan; now they have come for you, no one is left to speak up."*

---

[12] http://www.businessinsider.com/donald-trump-today-meredith-hawaii-video-2011-4

15

Jane Sanders in Arizona

Mary Jane O'Meara Sanders is easily the most involved candidate's significant other so far in these ongoing electoral campaigns. Not since Hillary Rodham Clinton in the 1990s have we seen such a spouse-cum-surrogate. The former president of Burlington College in Vermont is soft-spoken and gets her points across effortlessly. Mrs. Sanders is not the trophy wife we see but never hear; she is a woman of substance who could easily run for political office. Like her husband, she is not beholden to fancy dressing. She looks like you would see her if you just dropped in for a cup of water. She features on campaign circuits and gives interviews like no other spouse; 2016 Bill Clinton does not come close to this super spouse and super surrogate.

Apropos, I have not seen Bill Clinton anywhere on TV lately, and the media outlets are not missing him! I have heard someone on some cable news offer that the Hillary camp might have asked him (Bill) to stay in the shadows to avoid any unforced blunder. I agree: Y2K Bill is not 2016 Bill; neither is he the Bill of Obama 2012.

When Jane Sanders appeared on the network news this Saturday, I took time off my weekend agenda to note my appreciation of what she was doing for her man. She is indeed a personification of the saying that behind every successful man is a woman: she is the pillar of Bernie's bonanza. No wonder he abruptly ended an interview in Flagstaff, Arizona when the reporter insisted on raising questions about the wife's activity earlier in the week. He would rather protect her that way than help national news hunters to give vent to an incident involving her. Though Bernie campaign later said the reporter's time was up, it was obvious Bernie did not want his wife dragged into the sty.

What happened? On Thursday, March 17, a reporter from the local NBC affiliate Brahm Resnick asked Sanders about an encounter between notorious Arizona Sheriff Joe Arpaio and his wife Jane. Sanders unloaded tersely:

> "What Joe Arpaio is doing is an outrage. My wife went to look at the so-called Tent City, which is something that should not exist. The fact that he crashed her meeting is, to me, very, very wrong, not something he should have done. Thank you very much."

With the camera still rolling, Sanders stood up, unhooked his microphone abruptly, and walked out without any goodbyes. The encounter made national news because no one recalled the last time a candidate walked off the set of a booked interview. If the agreed time was up, Sanders could have ended it better. The next-day clarifications and corrections by his campaign did not hold much water; the trains had left the station.

Why did Sanders' people entangle with the dreaded sheriff that appears like the lifetime governor of Maricopa County, Arizona? Sheriff Joe Arpaio craves controversies. He will make obnoxious statements to get national media attention to his disrespect of federal immigration laws. He is the architect of Tent City, an open concentration camp where he practically fries prisoners in over 120-degree desert heat, where captives wear degrading pink underwear and eat morbid meals.

From what pundits have written about the man and the ongoing case of federal contempt for violating a judge's ruling not to enforce the "Paper Please" law that entails racial profiling, he could be the only openly racist law enforcement officer in all of USA. Sheriff Arpaio injected himself into Mrs. Sanders' itinerary, a visit designed to highlight the pitiful plight of illegal immigrants by the Mexican border. Here is his tweet:

> Jane Sanders came to tents jail, so I invited her inside so I could defend my tent policy. Now waiting for Hillary.
> 8:47 PM - 14 Mar 2016   Joe Arpaio_@RealSheriffJoe

I totally disagree with those who think that Mrs. Sanders should stay home and bake cookies. Reports have it that the civil rights group Puente planned the visit to draw national attention to the predicament of inhumanly incarcerated, illegal immigrants. This was where it should have stopped. Accepting and going with the sheriff for a tour of the inside of his infamous concentration camp was not worthwhile. I watched the encounter on television: Mrs. Jane Sanders held her own when the man injected his publicity-seeking self into her tour of the frying facility.

Once the basics cleared about who was backing whom—as if we did not know that Arpaio was Trump's trooper, she got more than she had bargained: meet with inmates of the Sheriff Arpaio's strange jail. The visit and the encounter brought back to public view the atrocious treatment of inmates of probably the only open desert jail in the world. Political correctness must take a backseat: this is simply inhumane; savages do not treat their kind with such savagery!

I was in Phoenix, Arizona on July 7, 2007. At 10.00 PM, the temperature outside was a blistering 110-degree Fahrenheit—better imagined than experienced. To have 8,000 prisoners in canvas tents in summer temperatures of 130 ºF is a scandal. Arpaio's argument that "the men and women out fighting for our country" in far-flung fronts of bloody battles also live in tents toys with common sense. If the only thing Mrs. Sanders did was to bring the matter to national attention, she accomplished her mission. She tweeted after the visit:

> I asked about racial profiling, 'Papers Please,' and
> deputizing civilians to round up undocumented people.
> He declined to answer.
>
> <u>10:52 PM - 14 Mar 2016</u> Jane O'Meara Sanders_
> @janeosanders

If Senator Sanders becomes the Democratic Party nominee and wins in November, America will have a first lady who makes her precursors look like handbags … with the exception of Eleanor, Hillary, and Michelle. A Roman Catholic married to a Jew and a top college administrator, we will read more about this woman warrior before the caucuses and primaries conclude.

16

Five Palm Sunday Finalists

This weekend, it appears everyone is in Arizona, the land of Barry Goldwater, except Hillary—who has been MIA on campaign circuits. She is busy raising big money in preparation for the epic battle with Trump—if he makes it out of Cleveland, OH in July. Senator Sanders is in the state, following his wife's preparatory visit during which she ran into an ambush by a controversial county sheriff. Senator Ted Cruz is by a Mexican-US border community in Arizona with former rival and now supporter Carly Fiorina.

Ohio Governor John Kasich insists on all the interviews he has been giving to the national media that the people are only now hearing him. He appears to believe in being a better option to Trump, not Ted Cruz —whom he apparently considers a nonstarter nominee. Kasich has ruled out being anyone's vice president, just as Speaker Ryan Paul has ruled out being a compromise convention candidate. On the later, we had heard of such denials before he took the speaker position; on the former, Trump may have to revisit the refusal down the road because Republicans need Ohio to win.

Mr. Trump continues to dominate the media with an estimated two billion dollars of free ads. Which begs the question, why does anyone want Trump to change a strategy that works so well? Why should he stop lampooning reporters and talking tough about punching protesters? Trump is not doing enough to lower the temperature in the Republican primaries. He has an endless list of persons and groups to denounce.

On the last Friday in Lent, in majority Mormon state of Utah, Trump continued his trademark tirades, questioning Romney's faith as he had done to Carson and Cruz: "Do I love the Mormons? I have many friends that live in Salt Lake City—by the way; Mitt Romney is not one of them. Are you sure he's a Mormon? Are we sure? He choked. He choked. It's so sad." Romney is a bishop of the Mormons, the Church of Jesus Christ of Latter-day Saints, though typical American Christians do not consider Mormons Christian enough.

The level of violence ratcheted up a bit yesterday, Friday, from the mild demonstrations in Salt Lake City. In Fountain Hill, AZ, protesters blocked roadways to stop people from driving to Trump's rally in 90 ºF heat, but it happened with only three arrests. Controversial former Governor Jan Brewer (R-AZ) attended with the host, Joe Arpaio. Over in Tuscan, AZ, I watched another episode of violence, where a Trump supporter punched and kicked a protester while he was on the ground. The authorities promptly arrested and charged the villain. The poor victim counted his blessings with no regrets. Trump's campaign manager Corey Lewandowski again got physical as if he were a bouncer. He will get a pass, again, but he may cross the line before long.

No matter how we slice it or spice it, Trump is on the way to getting the required 1237 delegates count before the Convention. To turn around and deny him the nomination by any means will be undemocratic. The reality has not stopped establishment Republicans from trying to rally around Senator Cruz—just to stop Trump, not that Republicans want as their nominee the creepy Christian fundamentalist and junior senator from Texas. They have no way out of the quagmire. Trump is cruising to victory. A bright spot in the cloud: Trump is a dealmaker. He will do the needful once he gets the numbers. Republicans will take Mama McCain's medicine and adopt him as their leader. He could throw them some bones, their choice of his vice president, and he may offer such top cabinet positions as defense, state, and treasury to technocrats.

Trump is an enigma. No one is knows what he will do with power, the ultimate aphrodisiac. For a New Yorker with an ego the size of Switzerland and all its wealth, Trump with power will be different from what we know about him. In fact, the only thing sure about Trump presidency is a surprise.

In an *Oprah* interview from two decades ago and trending on Facebook and WhatsApp via YouTube, Trump told Oprah Winfrey that he would run and win to stop countries ripping off America. Japan was then the chief culprit. China has since replaced Japan. No one knows what will become of Trump as president of USA, except that it would be a challenge. Abraham Lincoln should know; he posited, "Nearly all men can stand adversity, but if you want to test a man's character, give him power." Americans are tempted to test Trump.

I note the pushback from the Goldwaters on the comparison of their patriarch Barry Goldwater and Donald Trump, including the offering that Mitt's father, George Romney, did the same thing to Barry Goldwater as Mitt Romney is doing to Trump. From all accounts, written online or in videos, there are some similarities: the Republican establishment embraced both men with shields of thorns, and their white-power campaigns abused and badmouthed minorities. Yet, from what I gather, there are differences that make Trump no Goldwater. Goldwater was a US Republican senator and a different kind of conservative. Trump engages in populist appeals, in "commonsense conservatism," he claims. Trump is not a conservative Republican; he is more of a libertarian with an acute sense of profit in business, where winning justifies the means.

Trump may be courting believers in the ideals of Barry Goldwater, but he is no Barry Goldwater—and he knows it. Mrs. Susan Levine, née Goldwater, phoned into MSNBC's *Morning Joe* and stated, "Barry would just absolutely go crazy if he were watching this today. He would be yelling at the television. He would think it's embarrassing this situation we have with Donald Trump. It's not the Republican Party or the country that we knew 25 or 30 years ago."

Meanwhile, reports have it that Barry Goldwater Jr., an ex-Congressman (R-CA) supported the sister's assertion that the comparison of Trump with their father was troubling: "I don't think there's any comparison at all with Barry Goldwater. Donald Trump is an authoritarian. Barry Goldwater had principles and he was a gentleman. Donald Trump is a cowboy."

A neuroscience study on brainwave reactions during the Republican debates showed that TV viewers reacted more to Trump than the other candidates. A media-watch program on CNN offered reasons and alluded to his mastery of TV during his gig in NBC's reality show, *Apprentice.* I disagree: It has everything to do with the two billion dollars of free advertisements, the exceptional treatment of Trump's travels, and the media sticking him out in a field of not-so-popular wannabes. The broad coverage of Trump is yet to ebb; even when he takes a brief break, it is "breaking news" —as are his tweets at dawn. The outbursts of violence at his events are a part of the packaging, as evidenced by the involvement of his campaign manager Cory in the "lovefest" —according to Trump.

As the week of Easter rolls in, all eyes interested in politics are on the statewide primary elections for Democrats (Arizona, Alaska, Idaho, Hawaii, Utah, and Washington) and for Republicans (American Samoa— with no delegates to award, Arizona, and Utah). Clinton's camp mirrors the Sanders' strategy in sending Hillary's husband, former President Bill Clinton, to Tuscan, AZ to speak with supporters in preparation for the arrival of Hillary tomorrow. She should get a bigger chunk of the 75 Democratic delegates, regardless of Sanders' elevated efforts in the state. Trump should take the 58 Republican delegates in Arizona Republican's winner-takes-all rule. In Utah, the situation is different for Republicans: a candidate needs 50% of the votes to take it all; else, a complicated formula of awarding delegates applies. The Democrats will award delegates to the two major partakers: Bernie and Hillary.

Many Americans do not know that about 1,640 candidates filed formal statements of candidacy with the Federal Election Commission, FEC, according to *Ballotpedia*.[13] Some suspended their campaigns (as did 4 Democrats and 14 Republicans so far). Others like Vice President Joe Biden and Senator Elizabeth Warren (Democrats), and Mitt Romney and Rep. Peter King (Republicans) resisted the urge to take the next step.

Today, CNN features a Libertarian candidate for the presidency, former Governor Gary Johnson of New Mexico. He is not alone; about 14 others are in the race to become the party's nominee. Why we never get to see their debates or their rallies proves once more that the media outlets invest in the two main political parties that pull in the crowds and the cash. It is more an economic design than a political decision. Alas, if the people do not know about the other parties, and no one asks about them in polling, how is anyone to emerge from the outfield of political nowhere?

Gary Johnson posits that many Americans are Libertarians: economic conservatives and social liberals. This explains partly why Trump fascinates. Trumpism could be the shakeup that Republican Party needs to be more inclusive. Therefore, all the anti-Trump coalition may do well to back off and allow Trump to win the civil war decisively and force a deal between the victor and the vanquished. Republicans must loosen the grip of Christian fundamentalists and stay true to economic conservatism. Win or lose in November, this could be one of the benefits of Trump candidacy.

---

[13] https://ballotpedia.org/Main_Page

17

President Obama in Cuba

Today is Palm Sunday, March 20, 2016. President Barack Obama goes to Havana, Cuba. He will be the first sitting POTUS to visit the island nation since Calvin Coolidge came on a ship nearly 90 years ago, and Cuba is just swimmable 90 miles off the coast of Florida, USA. Watching Obama and family embark Air Force One, the presidential plane, reminded me of Richard Nixon going to China in 1972, and China is still a communist country.

Cuba-USA conflict is a direct consequence of mismanaged cold-war intervention by the otherwise great administration of John F. Kennedy. Why it lasted this long is another story. An urban legend that an Internet meme would want us to believe claims the Fidel Castro said in 1973: *"The United States will come talk to us when it has a black president and the world has a Latin American pope."* If these remarkable events are what it took to happen, the "prophesy" is fulfilled. Those who started it and led the battles are gone or passing on. Ernesto "Che" Guevara is long gone, and the Castro brothers will not be in power much longer.

The children born after the Bay of Pigs invasion of Cuba by ill-prepped Cuban exiles have grown into power, and they are not taking it anymore. Obama is one of them. Camilo Guevara, son of Che Guevara, is also of Obama's era, the early 1960s generation. In an interview with *The Guardian*, Camilo captured the shifting mood on the other side of the divide:

> "I don't know Obama in person. He appears intelligent and sensitive towards the major problems of humanity, but he came to power in an election, not a revolution. He was supported by corporate America. The colour of skin is one thing; the colour of ideology is another."

> "It's a historic and very important visit. It's the first time a US president will visit an independent Cuba. But the US is an empire. Their nature is not to set the table and invite you for a feast. History shows us that every time they set a table, you have to accept you might be poisoned or stabbed in the back. But let's see."

Yes, indeed, let's see.

Some say that a Republican president could reverse the changes. This is not likely. Guevara agrees, "The fact is that US-Cuba relations were stuck. Regardless of who becomes president next, things can't get any worse than they were in the past." Two Cuban Americans running for the presidency disagree only politically with the reopening of relationships. Rubio is out; Cruz is not about to overtake Trump in many of the remaining contests. Interestingly, Trump is not against opening diplomatic channels with Cuba. His contention is that he will make a better deal, a willingness to renegotiate "the deal." Everything about Trump is about making deals. Cuba is no exception.

The Trump Organization may be the first multinational to build a five-star hotel in Guantánamo Bay and another by José Martí International Airport, Havana! Of course, Hillary Clinton will fast-track the development of good relations with Cuba. She will soak her rightful dues in helping to lay the foundation, which Secretary of State John Forbes Kerry delivered in the same Obama administration they both served.

Whatever happens, Cuba changes—for better or for worse—from this day henceforth. Once the genie of change leaves the bottle, no one can stop the constancy of change. The issue to address is how to carry along the majority of Cuban citizens who have long suffered under the communist system that lingered long after the Soviet Union unraveled. No nation has ever regretted progress, as long as modernity mirrors correct cultural crescendos.

In essence, President Barack Obama changes today and forever the dynamics of Cuba-USA relations. This is yet another checkmark in the long and growing list of a consequential presidency made more significant by the organized obstructionism by radical Republican partisans, the positioning of radio hate hosts, the Tea Partiers, the tiring Trump-led birthers, and southern Christian fundamentalists known as "evangelicals." Then there were sundry haters and conspiracy theorists.

It is a historic day. Obama must have been so thrilled that he tweeted on touchdown in Havana:

> *¿Que bolá Cuba?* Just touched down here, looking forward to meeting and hearing directly from the Cuban people.
> *1:22 PM - 20 Mar 2016 President Obama@POTUS*

Obama's detractors will concede that he has done what he said he would do. In his inaugural address on January 20, 2009, he said, "To those who cling to power through corruption and deceit and the silencing of dissent, know that you are on the wrong side of history, but that we will extend a hand if you are willing to unclench your fist." The Castro communists know they are on the wrong side of modern history. Obama extended a hand of friendship; Raul Castro unclenched his revolutionary fist. The rest has been history in the making since Obama made momentous changes in the US relationship with Cuba on December 17, 2014.

Ted Cruz wants to scrap Obama rapprochement and "liberate" Cuba. He contends that his father fought with Castro against Cuban dictator Fulgencio Batista, but Castro's heavies so "brutalized" him and his aunt they fled Cuba and found liberty in God's own country —USA! The story has a K-leg because his father arrived Austin, Texas three years before Castro ran Batista out of town on 1.1.59! Powerful people who try to get even for what happened to their fathers raise my eyebrows. Recall why President George W Bush went to war to remove Iraq's Saddam Hussein? Besides oil, defense contracts, phantom WMDs, and money trumping peace, in late September 2002, GW proclaimed to the world: "After all, this is the guy [Saddam Hussein] who tried to kill my dad." We now know how far that mission went! Fourteen years later, a Cuban-Canadian American, Senator Edward (Ted) Rafael Cruz, is talking about revenging some cooked-up harm that Fidel (not Raul) Castro did to daddy Rafael Bienvenido Cruz. He just lost my vote—if he gets to ask for it in November!

18

Tailgating the Trump Train

In bucolic communes where canines consume crap, they usually follow a blaspheming, brick-hauling, and big-bellied brute of a drunk: If he does not throw up, he will defecate. Americans finally found out today why the media obsess with Donald J. Trump. Americans should have known to follow the money. The fragrance of funds foretells the pigment of politics. Bottom line: It is always all about money.

Trump is a viewer's magnet; advertisers chase American TV viewers. Therefore, the $1.8 billion of free advertisement that the media have so far granted Mr. Trump[14] is a win-win blueprint for both. Media managers and Trump feed off each other in a simple symbiotic relationship. Irrespective of the many times and ways that Trump castigates and derides reporters covering him, they follow him, lap up his vomits, and inhale his noisome oral emissions without barking. The media operators are into Trump for what they can get. Sensing the scenario, Trump is doing his bit to keep up the mutually beneficial relationship.

---

[14] According to calculations by *The New York Times*

Until today, Monday, 3.21.16, political pundits have pretended to be investigating the Donald Trump phenomenon when it has been perching on his nose. I chuckled when John Kasich told Anderson Cooper on *CNN*, "God created pundits to make astrologers look accurate."

Bingo!

So, on the eve of yet another Tuesday primaries, the lovefest continues. With President Obama still in Cuba and making history, any gringo who thinks the media would focus on Obama has not understood the unspoken synergy between them and Trump. Someone will someday come up with the percentage of time allocated to Obama in Cuba and to Trump going to Washington, DC. Trump was in Washington, DC today to pander to AIPAC, the pro-Israel group, about Ivanka having a Jewish baby, meet with such top Republicans such as former Speaker Newt Gingrich who will show their faces at this time, and do some interviews. Of course, he did not forget to use the media to highlight his new real estate deal: The Trump International Hotel at 1100 Pennsylvania Avenue. The White House is just blocks away at 1600 Pennsylvania Avenue.

It surfaced today that the executive chair and CEO of CBS, Les Moonves, had let the cat left out of the bag on Monday, February 29: "There's a lot of money in the marketplace." He called the presidential campaign a "circus" and confessed, "It may not be good for America, but it is damn good for CBS." According to *The Hollywood Reporter,* during a speech at the Morgan Stanley Technology, Media, and Telecom Conference in San Francisco, Mr. Moonves said:

> "Man, who would have expected the ride we're all
> having right now? ... The money is rolling in and this is
> fun. I've never seen anything like this, and this [is]
> going to be a very good year for us. Sorry. It's a terrible
> thing to say. But, bring it on, Donald. Keep going."

Now we know that money drives the love-hate, mutually beneficial relationship between Trump and the media. The resignation of Melissa Harris-Perry from *MPH Show* on MSNBC now made much money sense. If she had known of the new media paradigm, she might still have a weekend show to call her own. In a letter she made public on Friday, February 26, Professor Harris-Perry wrote:

> "I will not be used as a tool for their purposes. I am not
> a token, mammy, or little brown bobble head. I am not
> owned by Lack, Griffin, or MSNBC. Here is the reality:
> our show was taken — without comment or discussion
> or notice — in the midst of an election season."

The professor-turned-television anchor somehow forgot that the media industry is primarily more about making money and keeping shareholders happy than making the audience happy and respecting the hard work of employees. Hard work does not necessarily make more money in media business; smart work rakes in the dough of advertisers. It was sad to see Melissa leave a space she had worked so hard to brand for four years: *MHP Show* on weekends. It reminded me of *Countdown with Keith Olbermann*. MSNBC dropped the intense show at its peak. When supposedly popular talk shows become inconvenient, despite their high ratings, networks yank the carpet. The beat goes on.

On Saturday, February 27, *MHP* was a no show! Enter Joy-Ann Reid. There was no announcement from the grapevine, or formally, that Mrs. Reid will replace MHP on weekends. Still, any observer of MSNBC's game of talk-show changing chairs could bet to a degree of certainty that the Brooklyn-born Joy-Ann Reid (née Lomena) was on her way up the ladder. Just as Dr. Rachael Maddow perfectly positioned herself to take over from Keith Olbermann (not the sporadic substitute Tamara Hall), Joy had positioned herself to be the next best African-American female face on MSNBC. No one came close to the daughter of a Congolese father, who did not stay—as did Barack's Kenyan father, and a Guyanese mother. Harvard-educated and until recently editor of both TheGrio.com and *The Reid Report,* (a blog), Joy brought an articulate, educated, and strong voice with a soft approach that appeals to the TV audience.

I have not been able to catch *The Reid Report* on the afternoon TV show slot that replaced Tamron Hall's *NewsNation* on MSNBC. No one I know missed the departure of *NewsNation*. Ms. Hall did a far better job on NBC's morning *Today Show* with Matt Lauer and Savannah Guthrie. Texan Tamron Hall would have accepted what MSNBC executives allegedly wanted of Melissa Harris-Perry:

> Now, MSNBC would like me to appear for four inconsequential hours to read news that they deem relevant without returning to our team any of the editorial control and authority that makes MHP Show distinctive.

19

Brussels Burning

Belgian police finally captured Salah Abdeslam, the last of Paris Massacre culprits, last Saturday, March 19, after four months of hiding in his Molenbeek, Brussels neighborhood. I knew that pussyfooting European police forces would be slow in mining expedient information from him. They were still heading to court to discuss extraditing him across the border to France—in the same European Union! This sort of sorry situation fuels Trump's terrible policy proposals on fighting terrorism —"waterboarding or worse," rounding up families of terrorists, and forcing Apple to grant backdoor entry to its iPhone system as demanded by the Federal Bureau of Investigation, FBI.

This morning, Tuesday, March 22, ISIS-affiliated bombers hit Brussel's Zaventem airport and, an hour later, Maelbeek metro station near the European Union headquarters. Over three scores perished; dozens more, wounded. The criminal mind is a devil's workshop. How does a tiny group of fanatics sit somewhere on this planet and plot to cause the civilized world so much pain with beastly and brutish bombings?

From 9/11, the shoe-bomber, the underwear bomber, the printer bomb, the suicide bombers, through blowing a Russian passenger plane off the skies to shooting up Paris and now flight departure lounge in Brussels, terrorists have indeed earned their name: terror maestros! The breaking news may not alter the projections of today's primaries, but it will surely boost support in Trump's anti-Muslim base and beyond. The relative ease with which ISIS strikes continental Europe, especially in areas with high Muslim populations in Belgium and France, encourages the pop thinking that violence is rooted in Islam. Whatever the motive of ISIS and regardless of the good intentions of mainstream Muslims, no sane soul denies that the most bloody and vicious of today's terrorists are Muslims.

As expected, Trump was the first out of the block with his tweets before cockcrow at dawn, while other candidates slept. He called into morning shows with his tirades, as if to control the day's news. On *Fox News*: "I would close up our borders to people until we figure out what is going on. Look at Brussels, look at Paris, look at so many cities that were great cities." *Today Show* on NBC: "Waterboarding would be fine and, if they could expand the laws, I would do a lot more than waterboarding. You have to get the information and you have to get it rapidly." On CBS: "You look at what just took place in Brussels, and that's peanuts compared to what's going to happen because we're not tough enough, and frankly, our leaders aren't smart enough. We have to have very strong borders." Trump appeared set to define and direct the narratives away from what else anyone wanted to make of Brussels burning.

The strategy, if it was so, did not fly high enough. Many pundits want to know what is really happening, not what Trump is thinking. The media houses did not resist this bomb from Ted Cruz: "We need to empower law enforcement to patrol and secure Muslim neighborhoods before they become radicalized." If this had come from Trump, no one would read it twice. First, there are no such strictly Muslim neighborhoods in America as in Belgium. The idea is porous.

Speaking at a political rally in Washington State, Hillary slammed the building of walls and shutting off people. She wondered how anyone would wall off the Internet! Instead, she told CNN's Wolf Blitzer, "We have to toughen our surveillance, our interception of communication." John Kasich did not support Trump's demonization of Islam; rather, he called for the building of alliances. Kasich wanted Obama to come back from Cuba. Cruz concurred; his odium for Obama did not have a part two—only one version! With Obama, Cruz ignored the rule of not criticizing the President while on a foreign soil; then again, Cuba is home to Cruz!

While soaking in all the news about Brussels and political kneejerk reactions, it is easy to miss that Trump has had opportunities to tell the world how he will tackle ISIS. In an interview with *The Washington Post* Editorial Board, Monday, March 21, 2016, Fred Ryan asked if Trump would nuke ISIS if he were the POTUS. For someone who had claimed to be a straight talker, it was a simple question, and it required a simple answer. Instead, Trump mumbled something snippy about not starting "the process of nuclear" because he is a "great counter-puncher." His response is worth reading:

> Remember, one thing that everybody has said, I'm a
> counter-puncher. Rubio hit me. Bush hit me. When I said
> low energy, he's a low-energy individual, he hit me first.
> He spent, by the way, he spent 18 million dollars' worth
> of negative ads on me.

Reminded that the interview was not about his petty political punches, which played out daily on live television, that the question was about using "a tactical nuclear weapon against ISIS," Trump offered the most curious comeback in recent television interviews. As if he was talking to a bunch of primary school pupils with acute attention deficit disorder (AADD), Trump took off from the center "by a lot":

> I'll tell you one thing: This is a very good looking group
> of people here. Could I just go around so I know who
> the hell I'm talking to?

It may seem bizarre at first, but it is not: Trump had mastered the art of dealing with the media: Talk fast over them, allow as little interruption as possible, say things they find juicy, and keep jumping around the issues, related or unrelated. It had worked so well in the past. It worked with the editors of *Washington Post*: they moved on to another topic.

Trump never answered the question about using the nuclear weapons against ISIS, or not. Apparently, he was either not prepped properly on the subject, or he really did not know the answer. Question: Will Trump be ready when next the question pops up? I doubt it! With the human resources presently at his service, he is not capable of handling such questions satisfactorily.

20

Cyberology

Watching Trevor Noah interview the Estonian Prime Minister, Taavi Rõivas, resolved one of my concerns about the slow embrace of the Internet in the country that gave life to the concept of cyberspace. "Revolution doesn't happen when society adopts new technologies–it happens when society adopts new behaviors."[15] Since 2007, people in remote Kenyan villages have been using *M-Pesa* (mobile money) to send and receive money to and from each other. In such countries as Bangladesh and Nigeria, mobile banking is far more popular than in the USA.

Ene[16] (2000) studied the impact of the Internet on society and proposed *Cyberology* as a social study of the cyberspace—a sort of sociology of the Internet. The medium continues to affect the way we do many things. It holds the key to breaking bureaucratic bulges and canning crass corruptions. Such issues as the hanging chads of the Y2K elections and the extending long lines at polling stations will erase with voting online.

---

[15] Clay Shirky, Here Comes Everybody, p. 160
[16] Ene, M. O., *Cyberology*, July 2000

Prime Minister Rõivas revealed that Estonia had done all that and much more. For a small country of 1.3 million people that emerged from the Iron Curtain of Soviet communism with decrepit infrastructure, the transformation to a digital society is astonishing. With simple cellphone clicks, Estonia eliminated cobwebs of bureaucratic barriers, clogs in the wheels of economic development, and cankerworms of corruption.

Estonia's eager embrace of e-governance and e-society means that it has digitized services, public and private. As Rõivas explained it tonight, every Estonian wired with a cellphone and a secure digital signature can perform all the activities that took hours and days in other countries. From registering businesses, paying taxes, and voting, immediate solutions are now only a few smartphone swipes or computer-keyboard clicks away from any corner of the earth with Internet access.

President Obama did not let the stellar successes of Estonia escape his attention. Speaking in Austin, TX, on March 11, he called on leaders in digital technology to "create safe, secure, smart systems for people to be able to vote much easier online."[17] Disenfranchisement of voters cannot sustain in a country where the number of people who vote is low. Any system that makes it more difficult to vote, as some Republicans canvass, will further reduce participation by minority populations. Any system that sits out the cyberological revolution is destined for the bin of history. Voting is no exception; democracy must go digital to remain relevant.

---

[17] https://www.whitehouse.gov/the-press-office/2016/03/14/remarks-president-south-southwest-interactive

Today, the Utah Republican Party launched the largest online voting exercise in the United States since Michigan Democrats introduced online voting in 2004.[18] Anyone who registered to vote by March 17 can vote online from anywhere on earth. The setup will improve the number of voters who participate. Voting fraud, where it exists, is far too low to pose problems. The important thing here is more the ease of voting and collation of results. Whatever the result of tonight's trial, it will not take twelve more years to make another move towards e-voting. It is surprising that Obama, the fêted savvy president who brought Blackberry, YouTube, Facebook, Twitter, Skype, etc. to the White House, did not move the needle farther to the future.

Americans living overseas participated in the primaries. The Democratic Party awarded 13 delegates to its members living in countries from Afghanistan to Vietnam. This year, between March 1 and 8, voting took place with "an unprecedented turnout, up 50% from 2008." In all, "34,570 voters cast their ballots from over 170 countries all around the world, through in-person voting, by fax, email, and post.... DA [Democrat Abroad] volunteers worked around the clock and around the world over the past two weeks to verify and count every ballot cast."[19] The exercise is commendable, but the method is so last-century. If all goes well in Utah tonight, imagine the ease and the reduced cost of voting from abroad in primary elections.

---

[18] http://www.wsj.com/articles/utah-republicans-open-caucuses-to-online-voters-1458324718

[19] http://www.democratsabroad.org/global_presidential_primary_results

It is interesting to note that Democrats living outside the US voted overwhelmingly for Bernie over Hillary (69%-31% or 9 pledged delegates to 5). The same group of voters voted for Obama in 2008. One would have expected expatriates to support an ex-secretary of state (foreign minister). Why they back Bernie in 2016 over Hillary is open to analyses. The main issue here is full participation and access to the civic charge of citizenship. With 50% jump in participation for Americans living abroad within eight short years, e-voting will definitely bring the numbers to near 100%. Other states could come on board in municipal elections and streamline the technological twists before the next two general elections. The outcome of e-voting in US elections will be simply revolutionary.

Prime Minister Rõivas foresaw no major cause for concern about e-voting or e-government. No system is without attendant problems. Many government services are already online and functional, from filing taxes and paying traffic court fines to job applications and business registrations. Who will forget *ObamaCare*, the Affordable Healthcare Act (ACA), albeit with initial technical twists and turns, for which Secretary of Health and Human Services Kathleen Sebelius (née Gilligan) eventually lost her job in 2014? ObamaCare has become a component of the cyberworld. If small Estonia could embrace e-voting for a decade without major problems, it will be a cakewalk for America, even with the quickly resolved and small snafu of ObamaCare rollout.

21

Results in, Gloves Out

Senator Sanders was disappointed with the results in Arizona. Campaign manager Jeff Weaver was taut and fire-eyed. He would have called for a recount, but the numbers were not close, almost 60-40 in Hillary Clinton's favor. With the comfortable wins in the caucuses of Idaho and Utah, Sanders' campaign desperately wanted to beat Mrs. Clinton in the desert state of Arizona. It was not to be; the Clintons had deep Democratic roots in Arizona. With this win, the gate is closing on the surprise surge by Sanders.

Ted Cruz's win among the Mormons of Idaho, Utah, and a county in Arizona came with another of his political abracadabra. An anti-Trump super PAC, 'Make America Awesome'—not necessarily pro-Cruz— made a targeted political attack advert for Utah Mormons. The ad featured a lacy and little-left-to-the-imagination nude photo of Trump's trophy wife Melania as a GQ model. The caption screamed:

MEET MELANIA TRUMP. YOUR NEXT FIRST LADY.
OR, YOU COULD SUPPORT TED CRUZ ON TUESDAY.

UK's *Daily Mail* called the ad "slut-shaming." Surely, it was offensive by any decent political standard. No real politician should use such a normal model pose of then Melania Knauss as a depiction of the real-life Mrs. Trump. The lie here is not that she featured in a near-nude pose—she did; the truth, however, is that she was a top model. If she were an ace pilot or an Olympic swimmer, I doubt an attack ad would use her photo in the appropriate gear. Trump was justifiably angry. Any man would defend his wife. Trump took to his favorite Twitter platform: "Lyin' Ted Cruz just used a picture of Melania from a G.Q. shoot in his ad. Be careful, Lyin' Ted, or I will spill the beans on your wife!"

Trump was losing the state in a winner-takes-all stake. Cruz must have known that his camp overplayed its hands. He took to damage control without waiting for the dust to settle: "Pic of your wife not from us. Donald, if you try to attack Heidi, you're more of a coward than I thought. #classless." In such fights, no hold is barred. The die is cast. Trump does not take a hit without giving back. He calls it "counter-punching."

Many folks on WhatsApp get unflattering photos and memes of Mrs. Melania Trump. One meme featured Melania and Ivana (Trump's ex) with a caption alluding to their being immigrants (from Czech and Slovenia respectively) and doing the job Americans will not do! It is indeed interesting that Trump favored East European women twice for marriage. *Is he afraid of the "one-drop (of black blood) rule"?* Another meme compared Melania's model poses to what *Fox News* said about Mrs. Michelle Obama baring her lovely arms and wondered what Fox would do with Melania as First Lady that bared all.

Mrs. Cruz did not see what beans there were to spill about her. What could she have done that was as impeachable as posing nude for glossy magazines? On Wednesday night, Trump could no longer hold back on his threat to hit back—forget "spilling beans"; there was nothing to spill: Heidi said so while campaigning for her husband in Wisconsin. Most conveniently, someone tweeted a meme made with a glamor-glitzy, polished-face photo of model Melania vis-à-vis, as in comparison, a faultfinding photo of Heidi Cruz and captioned it: "No need to 'spill the beans.' The images are worth a thousand words." Trump retweeted the meme tweet.

Retweeting has become the cyber-equivalent of 'I endorse this message.' This was how the fight escalated. Within the hour last evening, Ted Cruz or someone staffing his Twitter account tweeted "Donald, real men don't attack women. Your wife is lovely, and Heidi is the love of my life." Nice! Today, 3.24.16, Ted Cruz could not hold back anymore. He thundered to some TV reporters, "Donald, you are a sniveling coward; leave Heidi the hell alone." It was going so deep into the gutsy gutter that Megyn Kelly, who should be stepping out of Trump radar, stepping right into in with an I-had-said-so tweet: "Seriously?"

To those who thought the presidential campaign shenanigans could not get any lower, this development must not come as a surprise. It has been in the works. In a flagrant display of double standard, pundits did not flinch when Trump attacked President Bill Clinton, not on his record, but as the spouse of Hillary, his political opponent. What does Bill's peccadillo, for which the House impeached him, have to do with Hillary?

Bill's indiscretion with Monica Lewinsky was public knowledge and ancient story. For Trump to use it in an anti-Hillary attack is as fair an attack as showing the publicly available and near-nude photos of his wife as a model. In a reversed situation, say Hillary is Bill, and Bill is Hillary, pundits would condemn Trump for strengthening his misogyny.

Pulling pettiness from the bottom rack of news articles never allows for civility in political discourse. Ted Cruz was so vexed he vowed to beat Trump for the nomination. Without saying it, he made it clear that the previous accord to support the Republican nominee is off the table. This is understandable: When you attack a man's mother, his wife, and or his children, you declare a lingering war. That Jeb Bush endorsed Ted Cruz did not come as a surprise; it only tells that the Bushes will not vote for Donald Trump, if he emerges the nominee.

Last night with Trevor Noah on Comedy Central's *Daily Show,* and this morning on MSNBC with *Morning Joe's* Mika Brzezinski, Senator Lindsey Graham continued his strange surrogacy for Senator Ted Cruz. Confronted with his choosing poison over shooting, he wisecracked that an antidote to poison was possible. On supporting Ted Cruz only because he was not Donald Trump, the senator from South Carolina could hold back no more: "My party is completely screwed up." Indeed, the Republican Party is in a serous quandary. The romance with political extremism yielded a large army of angry white men and women waiting for a generalissimo. Trump popped up with a train, and they boarded. The train has now taken off firmly on the sure tracks to an uncertain chaos in Cleveland.

Dr. Carson, now surrogating for Trump, found himself in the same scratchy situation as Graham. Whoopi Goldberg took him to task about endorsing Trump, a man that compared him to a child molester:

> "I hate to ask this question, but you have aligned yourself with a man who has bashed women, made countless racist remarks. And you're Ben Carson! Why would you align yourself with that?

Carson is not easily rattled, but the women of ABC's *The View* –especially Whoopi and Joy Behar—put him on the spot. His lame response again alluded to the bipolarity of Trump's persona: "You have to look at the good and the bad." He agreed that Trump lied about him, but posited that all politicians lie. It was a painful encounter, very much so that Trump took to Twitter to condemn the show he had appeared on as a guest.

It appears that the media houses are entering the reality zone. Pundits now express surprise that Trump is indeed heading to the 1237-delegate count, and it may be too late to stop him. Yet, they cannot stop talking about Trump, whose unfavorable rating with women (53% of voters) is between 50 and 70%. From polls, the only candidate capable of beating Hillary in the general election is Governor John Kasich of Ohio.

Meanwhile, President Obama vowed in Cuba, "We will do whatever is necessary to support our friend and ally Belgium in bringing to justice those who are responsible." Criticisms of his continuing with the trip to Argentina, dancing the tango and not altering the details of his trip, did not stick. Obama put a lock on it: "The terrorists want to disrupt our lives."

Obama is past caring what his traducers think. He focuses on the agenda he has set for the remainder of his tenure. In a very curious way, no one pauses to ponder why Obama has not visited Chicago as violence rages in his Windy City. Surely, the optics is not kosher: watching baseball as Brussels burns and dancing the tango in Argentina while American victims of terrorism are unaccounted. Sadly, people die every day in terror attacks all over the world. The ISIS-affiliate Boko Haram sect in northeastern Nigeria murders people regularly. Nothing stops. The anarchist Al Shabab in Somalia and those in northern Kenya terrorize the region regularly. In Afghanistan, Pakistan, Iraq, and Syria, terrorism has become a revolting way of life.

Ted Cruz's call for President Obama to return and head to Brussels smacks of political opportunism. If that is what he will do as president, then he has no business running for the office at this time. For making such a silly statement, Trevor Noah called Cruz a "sanctimonious jackass." Mr. Herman (999) Cain dusted up and lent his hollow voice on Twitter: "Obama does 'the wave' with the mass-murderer who tried to kill my father-in-law." By the way, is it still not the rule that no politician criticizes the president while on a foreign soil?

Breaking News from Brussels' bombing filtered into news coverages, but the campaigns still dominated. There was also the matter of clarifying the phantom Biden Rule. Vice President Joe Biden pooh-poohed the selective quoting of Senator McConnell. In a speech at Georgetown University Law Center today, he said, "It's frankly ridiculous...there is no Biden Rule."

Yep, none!

22

Derailing Donald Trump's Train

ood Friday, March 25, 2016: The Trump train still looks unstoppable. The Republican Party establishment, a group of traditional members also called "establishment republicans," is yet to come up with a plausible plan worth repeating. No path to overtaking Trump in the delegate count exists, let alone another candidate making the 1237 mark before July. The only option open at this time is a possible contested convention, assuming Trump does not lock up state delegates of New York and California. Wisconsin appears to be the new battlefront. Governor Scott Walker is not supporting Trump, and Speaker Paul Ryan (R-WI) is not a fan of Trump.

No new top Republican came out to stump on 'stop Trump.' They forgot what Mahatma Gandhi said, "Silence becomes cowardice when occasion demands speaking out the whole truth and acting accordingly." Last Wednesday, March 23, while speaking on the state of American politics to a bipartisan group of interns at the House of Representatives, Speaker Paul Ryan said:

> We don't shut down on people—and we don't shut people down. If someone has a bad idea, we tell them why our idea is better. We don't insult them into agreeing with us. ::: Governing ourselves was never meant to be easy. This has always been a tough business. And when passions flair, ugliness is sometimes inevitable. But we shouldn't accept ugliness as the norm. We should demand better from ourselves; we should demand better from one another."[20]

Obviously, Trump got the gist without his name or anyone in the presidential primaries mentioned. Yesterday, March 24, he proposed a rally for next Tuesday in Janesville, WI, Ryan's hometown and a part of his congressional constituency. Ted Cruz, who talks about Muslims as pejoratively as Ryan has disapproved, also scheduled a Janesville appearance on Thursday to canvass for votes in the state's primary of April 5. With the love for Janesville, Paul Ryan's stock in a contested convention rises astronomically.

Despite Speaker Paul Ryan's denials of playing any role in determining the way forward, many political pundits view his position with reservation. He has been through such stages before. It appears he loves to be a beauty-full political bride. First, when he popped up as vice-presidential candidate to Romney, he presented such a carefree comportment many wondered why he bothered to accept. Then there was his reluctance to inherit Speaker John Boehner's chair. Ryan's resistance often dissolves under pressure. It could happen again, but this is Trump's time. Trump takes no hostages.

---

[20] http://www.speaker.gov/press-release/full-text-speaker-ryan-state-american-politics

President Obama has a way of silencing critics. He shows again that he can walk and chew gum, as he did in 2011 by sending troops to get Osama bin Laden while humiliating Trump at the annual White House Correspondents' Association dinner in Washington, D.C. This afternoon, Secretary of Defense Ash Carter announced from the Pentagon that US Special Forces eliminated the chief financial officer of ISIS, Abd al-Rahman Mustafa al-Qaduli, also known as Abu Ala al-Afri. The man had a $7-million tag on his head. The plan was to capture him, but something went wrong.

While Obama seemingly parties in Argentina and decapitates the multi-headed monster called ISIS (or Daesh, as Secretary John Kerry now calls them), Cruz and Trump are busy talking about their wives and adultery. They are not bothered about what Belgium, France, and Germany are doing in Europe to stop ISIS terror agents at advanced stages of their plot to strike again. Only Hillary Clinton has been acting presidential, giving policy lectures and addressing security issues.

As if to deny anyone a space on television, the Internet erupts with a report in the *National Enquirer*, a supermarket-checkout tabloid, that Ted Crux has had numerous affairs. Ordinarily, no one takes such reports seriously. Why the trash tabloid found itself at the main table of political discourse belongs to the shady world of agents provocateurs preying on the dynamism of social media fueled by Trumpmania. If the so-called sex-scandal did not have a Trump angle to it, and Cruz did not mount a spirited denial before anyone asked, the story would have vamoosed with Easter eggs.

Irony of ironies and the apogee of arrogance, the duo of Cruz and Trump who wanted Obama to come back home or head to a closed Brussels airport forgot all about ISIS. Instead, they climbed down to the gutter of garrulous gossips and sleazy sex scandals. Politicians are predictable; they never fail to deliver inanities.

President Barack Obama will have the fun of his life during the last White House press dinner on April 30. Below are just four jokes I rustled up and shared on my Facebook page, which the comedian-in-chief could adapt and use as he pleases:

1. Did y'all see Speaker Ryan with Muslim-friendly beard? Look! [Shows photo on screen] 'Assalamu alaikum, Brother Rahman'!

2. Donald Trump… ah ya ya ya… he never gives up: Did you know that he sent investigators to Calgary, Canada to find out if Ted Cruz was foreign-born? Well, you will NEVER know the YOOGE facts they are finding out as I speak: By extraordinary executive powers, I have asked INS to deny the team reentry into USA--until after June 4th!

3. American politics has changed since I got here: Now you can scream all you want and still win your party's nomination. Secretary Hillary Clinton owes Governor Howard Dean an apology!

4. Bernie! I like Senator Sanders: His father was born in Poland, a Jew--as was mine in Kenya, a Muslim. How come no one is asking for his birth certificate? Hello Tea-bag Birthers! This is age discrimination. Not fair, not fair at all!

I also note that Dr. Rachael Maddow deserves a shout-out for her work on Flint, MI water scandal, and I wish 2016 host Larry Wilmore good luck on taking his *"de-negrofication* of White House" to mainstream media. We will surely miss Barack and Michelle Obama, and now-grown Obama princesses... and the First Grandma. This is indeed a good time to be alive.

23

"Lyin' Ted" v. "Sleazy Donald"

Is sex scandal a killer of political prospects? Yes, but the location of, and the reaction to, the sex scandals bring down politicians more than the sex act itself. Americans are not snoopy in character… well, until the Kardashians and reality TV. So much is going on in America; the least many Americans want to know is who sleeps with whom under the sheets. Americans hate hypocrisy, the holier-than-thou attitude of invented role models. President Jimmy Carter once confessed: "I've looked on many women with lust. I've committed adultery in my heart many times. God knows I will do this and forgives me. [21]"

The height of hypocrisy was Republicans in the Congress pointing fingers at President Clinton for his *"it depends on what 'is' is"* issue with Monica Lewinsky. In the party's periscope, Clinton was the lowest of the low! Yet, their congressional leaders were involved in worse sex scandals. Ironically, the *cleanest* congress rep the Republican finally found and made Speaker, John Dennis Hastert, was a closet homosexual child molester!

---

[21] In a *Playboy* magazine interview, November 1976

Sex scandals seem to be a recurring ritual in American politics. Some are so bizarre that one cannot stop chin scratching and wondering, as Jay Leno asked Hugh Grant in 1995 (after Divine Brown affair), 'What the hell were they thinking?' In June 2009, Governor Mark Sanford (R-SC) disappeared from his own state. His whereabouts became a matter of some speculations. Six days later, reporters saw him at Hartsfield–Jackson Atlanta International Airport. It turned out that he had flown out to Buenos Aires, Argentina, to shack up with Maria Belén Chapur, an Argentine journalist.

What was he thinking!

Governor Mark Sandford's wife Jenny left him. He resigned, but he won an election to Congress in 2013 when Governor Nikki Haley (R-SC) elevated Tim Scott, an African-American congressional representative, to the senate seat vacated by James Warren "Jim" DeMint. Senator Jim DeMint had left the US Senate in January that year to preside over a conservative think tank called The Heritage Foundation.

In 2007, Senator David Vitter (R-LS) popped up in the books of a Washington, DC madam. It was not a new story; it confirmed accusations of his patronizing prostitutes made five years earlier. He apologized and let the storm blow over. He won reelection in 2010, but failed in a 2015 gubernatorial race in Louisiana. Who will forget Senator Larry Craig! In June 2007, at the Minneapolis–St. Paul International Airport, authorities arrested the Republican US Senator from Idaho for lewd conduct in a men's restroom. He refused to resign, entered a guilty plea to a lesser charge, failed to reverse the plea, and then bowed out of politics.

Just as Trump was twisting everyone's eyes to focus on a phantom sex scandal involving Ted Cruz—a co-candidate for high office, an actual sex scandal was unfolding live in the state of Alabama. Apparently, Governor Robert Bentley (R) was flirting with his closest aide and senior political adviser Rebekah Caldwell Mason. Despite salacious taping of what appears like phone-sex sessions, Mr. Bentley still swore that there was zero physical affair and apologized.

On Good Friday, the state auditor Jim Zeigler initiated an ethics investigation: "This is not about his personal peccadillos; it is about the improper use of state funds and the right of the people to know who is paying the advisors to our public officials." Oh yes, it is not about sex, just location. Really! Those who say the House of Representatives impeached Clinton because he lied to special prosecutor Kenneth Winston "Ken" Starr about Monica are telling a half-truth; it was about the location (Oval Office) and about trying to explain it! Watching Governor Bentley try tortuously to lighten an obvious sex scandal cracked me up: Politicians are poor students of history, and they are too slow to learn.

Sex is not the problem—as long as it is between two agreeable adults. Adultery is not a public problem —if kept under wraps by the participants. The case of Hulk Hogan v. Gawker shows that Americans are not yet ready to allow the First Amendment's free-speech stipulations to impinge on the right for some privacy. The case is complicated but easy to understand. Hulk Hogan, an entertainment wrestler, had consensual sex with a friend's wife on tape. Gawker streamed the tape on line. He sued. The case is ongoing in a Florida court.

Gawker is a New York City-based blog founded in 2003; it focuses on news and gossips about celebrities. Millions of gawkers visit the site every month. The media group crossed the line in 2012 by showing 101 seconds of the sex tape depicting 62-year-old Hulk Hogan and Heather Clem in the act. Hogan sued for emotional distress and gross violation of privacy. Gawker says it received the 30-minute tape from an anonymous source and published some seconds of the intimate act claiming First Amendment right. To Hogan, the emotional pain and the loss of privacy are worth a whopping $100 million.

Comparing Hogan's case with the phone-sex tape of Governor Bentley, I wonder when Bentley will sue to get his own 100-million dollars for unnecessary humiliation on MSNBC's *TRMS*! Rachel Maddow does not seem to care. With the (in)famous TNYT v. Sullivan, it is hard for a politician to win a case of defamation. Politicians no longer bother to sue. The monkeyshines of President Franklin D. Roosevelt (FDR) did not diminish his legend, and his wife Eleanor, an acclaimed activist, made no fuss. The tales of President John F. Kennedy (JFK) and model Marylyn Monroe did not detract from the successes of his presidency.

The modern departure from keeping private matters private probably dates back to 1988 presidential primaries. Democratic candidate, Senator Gary Hart (D-CO) was set to become the nominee. There were rumors of his love for beautiful young women, but American hardworking public let sleeping dogs be. Certain things were better left where they belonged. Presidential candidates are humans, and no one is a living saint.

However, when *Miami Herald* revealed that the married man had been spending time with a beauty-full model named Donna Rice, the media went for his jugular. Senator Hart made matters worse: He failed to come clean with an apology to his family. He deployed image-makers to control the damage and save his quest for power. His reaction backfired—as usual.

"Have you ever committed adultery?" That was one heck of an easy question at that point, knowing what he knew—that the tabloids most likely knew a lot more. The near-saint Jimmy Carter had answered the same question unasked in a *Playboy* interview in 1976: "I've looked on a lot of women with lust. I've committed adultery….." Mr. Hart failed to answer, and the media went to work. It turned out that Gary and Donna had been living *la dolce vita*. Back in June 1987, a *National Enquirer* cover photo showed the same Donna Rice on the Senator Hart's laps aboard a yacht named, wait for it, "Monkey Business"! The dude chose a bad location. On May 8, 1988, Hart threw in the towel and ended a surefire sojourn in the White House.

It is a long way from Gary Hart and Donna, punctuated only by Bill Clinton's sex scandal in 1998. Before Monica Lewinsky, before the Clintons made it to the White House, sex scandals shadowed the couple from Arkansas. With his wife Hillary Rodham Clinton "standing by my man like Tammy Wynette," Bill beat back kiss-and-tell model Jennifer Flowers. People close to Bill Clinton knew all about him and hookers. The tabloids were on top of the stories, and Ms. Flowers did not hold back. Yet, the American public elected and reelected Bill Clinton as president.

In December 2007, as if Bill Clinton's shenanigans were stellar successes, former UN Ambassador Andrew Young volunteered without solicitation, "Bill [Clinton] is every bit as black as Barack. He's probably gone out with more black women than Barack." He admitted that he was "clowning," but Young told a story I had read.

Which brings us to a *taste* of checkout counter rags. I was in a London Safeway supermarket in 1992. The cover of a tabloid held my attention: Bill Clinton has a son, and he is black! The Brits do not commonly use "black" as in America. I picked up a copy. It was not just a story; the boy's photo was there. The faces compared. Oh, the mother spoke! Where I come from, a woman knows the father of her son… well, until Maury Povich proved that 101% certainty equals to 0% chance!

The Clinton story came full circle in 2013. The *Globe*, the same tabloid, followed up on the story I had read 21 years before in London. Love child Danney Lee Williams Jr., now 27 and a father of five, wanted Bill Clinton to see his grandchildren! True or false, such stories do not usually make it to the television, and few mainstream media go down the valley of voyeurism for a glimpse of *garbage*, or so they say.

In an election cycle featuring Donald Trump, and if anyone was supposed to inject a small semblance of sex-scandal, the Donald is it. He did not disappoint. He lobbed the Monicagate missile. It is an old story, but many under-30 voters do not know of the story. The missile did not fly. Trump said it was to counter the anti-women missiles from Hillary. That done, he zeroed in on Ted Cruz: *The National Enquirer* story about his sex life came from the dark alleys, but it rattled Cruz.

Cruz was quick to call the story "garbage" and accuse "Donald Trump and his henchmen" of planting it. He was understandably angry, but a more mellowed laugh-off would have been more appropriate, or a complete disregard. Then again, he wears the shoes. He feels the pinch. He presents himself as a man afraid of something. If he has zilch to hide, and no truth in the tabloid tale... as is so far the case, Cruz could have held back on open accusation of Trump as the source.

Cruz forgot that Trump thrives in such sleaze. In Trump's world, no publicity is bad publicity—as long as it is about him. The more people talk about anatomical extremities, mistresses, and wives, the more Trump avoids such substantive subjects as security, economy, and education. He fakes it until he makes it.

Trump's camp denied outright the charge of any participation in producing and or propagating the story. Trump's statement is revealing and tells a whole lot more than meets the eye:

"I have no idea whether or not the cover story about Ted Cruz in this week's issue of the *National Enquirer* is true or not, but I had absolutely nothing to do with it, did not know about it, and have not, as yet, read it. I have nothing to do with the *National Enquirer* and unlike Lyin' Ted Cruz I do not surround myself with political hacks and henchman and then pretend total innocence. Ted Cruz's problem with the *National Enquirer* is his and his alone, and while they were right about O. J. Simpson, John Edwards, and many others, I certainly hope they are not right about Lyin' Ted Cruz. I look forward to spending the week in Wisconsin, winning the Republican nomination and ultimately the presidency in order to Make America Great Again."

Trump's denial did not only sound hollow, it also talked up the paper, with which he was allegedly associated. In the process, he recounted instances where the notorious tabloid supposedly got it right, as if to alert the public that no smoke pops up without fire.

Beyond Trump's glowing interviews in, and contributions to, the paper, Cruz informed: "[T]he CEO of the *National Enquirer* is an individual named David Pecker, who is a good friend of Donald Trump going back many years," and the paper has endorsed Trump to be president, rain or shine. If Trump was not directly involved in the exposé, he probably knew more than he was ready to admit. He knew that some scandal was cooking for Cruz. Many people in the cybercommunity, the surfers of social media—as is Trump, had read of the rumors coming from various obscure sources under the hashtag #CruzSexScandal.

While speaking with reporters, Cruz accused a certain Mr. Roger Stone, a former adviser and an ally of Trump, of "foreshadowing that this attack was coming." Stone, known for such shady schemes and for which he and Trump parted ways, did not deny foretelling the scandal. Read Ted Cruz:

> "And I would note that Mr. Stone is a man who has 50 years of dirty tricks behind him. He's a man for whom a term was coined for copulating with a rodent. Well, let me be clear: Donald Trump may be a rat, but I have no desire to copulate with him."

It appears that Ted Cruz is taking off the gloves finally. He is no longer folding as Trump tries to eat both his breakfast and lunch. It will be his dinner soon and the game will be over. He fired on:

> And so Donald, when he is losing, when he is scared, when Republicans are uniting against him, decides to peddle sleaze and slime. You know, Donald is fond of giving people nicknames, with this pattern he should not be surprised to see people calling him "Sleazy Donald" because that is his first and last redoubt, to turn to sleaze.

In an African parable of the Igbo folk, the fable-ubiquitous tortoise swore to stump a pregnant woman to death if a market stampede ensured. A stampede ensured, as they did often in large, open farm markets; those with huge legs trampled a poor pregnant woman to death. The community apprehended the tortoise, despite dynamic denials. Trump had vowed to "spill the beans"; someone went ahead and did it. Trump has no chance of walking away from the filth of his politics. Alas, unless something more atrocious than standing on 5th Avenue and shooting someone happens, Trump will get a pass from the people who profit from his lows.

Pained by the trash, 'courageous conservative' Cruz stopped inches of declaring that he would never vote for 'commonsense conservative' Trump: "I don't make a habit out of supporting people who attack my wife and attack my family. And Donald Trump is not going to be the Republican nominee." The lesson is very simple: He who plays with chickens always has chicken poop on his hand, and a rat does not follow a lizard into a pond. Anyone who has followed Trump down the deserted *Dirty Dozen Driveway* ends up on a constricted cul-de-sac, a dead end. While Trump the tiger was eating up everyone, Cruz cruised the southern plains savoring the smell of smoldered souls. The list of Trump's victims is long. Cruz's turn has come.

The plot of Cruz camp was to inherit the tiger's kills after some phantom hunter had killed the tiger. Unfortunately, for the tortoise in Ted Cruz, the tiger has eaten all the known hunters, with two left to go. Cruz had enjoyed the tiger's rides gleefully for many moons. When it got to Ted's turn in Texas, he woke up and jumped off the tiger's back. Alas, he rode the tiger for far too long before dismounting. The tiger is now facing him and nibbling at his foot. Whether he ends up eaten or survives, he will never be the same again.

Chairman Mao nailed it nicely when he posited, "Politics is war without bloodshed, while war is politics with bloodshed." Any war is raw. Partisan politics is not for the fainthearted. In a forward position of play, it is either you eat someone, or someone eats you as lunch. In politics, no frontrunner surrenders, none retreats: either you win, or you learn to play a healthier hand. Trump is poised to devour his opponents by any means possible—fair or foul. He has learned enough.

Of sex and scandals, Donald J. Trump is an embodiment, but the media apparently consign them to the news backburner as they embrace his endless antics. It also appears as if late-night comedians are indirectly rooting for Trump. For all the fine woods that the media gather from the obvious political television reality show, comedians could cook a feast for America. The media magically suppress all talks about policies as they chase Trump across the country and feed off his rambling repetitive mantra about making America great again. When we wake up from the media-induced magic land of uninterrupted abracadabra, it will be too late to pull out the lone nut from a raging fire.

24

Curious Katrina

The only visible African American in Trump's team, Katrina Pierson is a stimulating surrogate. I first noticed the young woman this January in a CNN interview. The network labelled her a 'national spokesperson for Trump campaign.' My eyes lit up. She looked relatively young to occupy such high office for a high profile candidate as Mr. Donald Trump. She sounded stable in her convictions. Her liveliness reminded me of Mary Matalin, James Carville's wife and opposite alter ego. She was without Mrs. Carville's depth and decorum, but she was good. Of course, an elder that sends a child to catch a shrew should provide the water with which s/he will wash the hands

The issue at stake was a sarcastic statement she had tweeted during the 2012 presidential elections: "Perfect Obama's dad born in Africa, Mitt Romney's dad born in Mexico. Any pure breeds left?" CNN's Brian Stelter of *Reliable Sources* asked if she wished to retract the racially insensitive remarks. Ms. Pierson did not flinch. She seemed steady. Her robust response was immediate:

"No, not at all! Look, these tweets… I'm an activist, and I am a half-breed. I'm always getting called a half-breed. And on Twitter when you're fighting with liberals and even establishment, you go back at them in the same silliness they are giving you. So, I myself am a half-breed."

The gritty response was gusty and gobsmacking. What sort of clown-car politics was she playing putting down the two top candidates in 2012 and, in the process, herself? What nerve to call President Obama "Chief Negro" and ask of what he has done for Black people? A few clicks turned up that she served on the advisory committee of Texas Tea Party and rose to become somebody with the anti-Obama rednecks. Like President Obama, a white woman from Kansas gave birth to Katrina; both have fathers of African extraction. There ended the similarities. The rest is an unfolding result of political indoctrination and what Nigerians call 'stomach infrastructure'—food on the table.

Katrina has a checkered history, according to reports. She has overcome the difficulties of life in typical American zero-to-hero fashion. A graduate and a young mother, she reportedly supported Obama in 2008. She made a 180-degree turn thereafter and subscribed to the Tea Party philosophy. She worked in the 2012 Senate campaign of Ted Cruz. She ran for Congress in 2014 as "a feisty fighter for freedom" (Sarah Palin) and an "utterly fearless principled conservative" (Ted Cruz). She introduced Trump at a campaign rally in Dallas, Texas in September. By November 2015, she was Mr. Trump campaign's national spokesperson.

Not bad!

Ms. Pierson is set to go places. If Trump gets the Republican nomination, as is looking likely every day, she may be a regular feature on cable news. I have seen more mature appearances, where she held her ground with veteran talking heads. She actually sounds more informed and more persuasive than some airheads that pop up as flash surrogates for Mr. Trump. Her major problems are two-fold: her impeachable background and her easy eagerness to sacrifice the truth on the altar of political proxy.

Curiously, one of the five women mentioned in Ted Cruz's supposedly "sleaze and slime" sex scandal is this same sister, Katrina Pierson, Mr. Trump's national spokesperson. Did her work with Cruz go beyond pure professional relationship? Ms. Pierson declared in a tweet on Good Friday that "the *National Enquirer* story is 100% FALSE!!!" In case anyone mistakenly read that she was exonerating Cruz and impeaching Trump, she added, "I only speak to myself, however. Carry on...."

Ms. Pierson's politics presents her as loathsome to her traducers. To her haters, the sex scandal involved the *right* person in the political pigsty. The political flamethrower and self-styled communication consultant could have done a better job of denying her association in the scandal nudging at her former and current bosses. At times like this, when you do not have something solid to say, you say nothing; besides, Trump has issued a statement distancing his campaign from the slander. As flawed as it is, the Trump statement has addressed the matter. Twitter lingo apart, the piece below did not convince her traducers of her innocence:

What's worse? People who actually believe the trash in tabloids, or the ones who know it's false & spread it anyway? #stupidity on all levels
11:14 AM - 25 Mar 2016   ✓ *@KatrinaPierson*

Nice and clear? Nope! The story is just beginning. If Trump gets more scandals of this nature closer home, he may have to do some cleanup. There may be just one room for all sexual shenanigans: Trump's. Surrounding himself with scandal-prone people is a surefire street to gaining popular apathy. Sadly, as American political history shows, Democratic and Republican politicians are never too far from sex scandals.

Ms. Omarosa Manigault is another celebrity African-American woman prominent in Trump's train. She was formerly in *The Apprentice*, Trump's reality show about make-believe business deals. Omarosa, as popularly known, worked for former Vice President Al Gore, a Democrat. Now she is Trump's campaign Director of African-American Outreach.

Good luck with that, sistah!

25

Socialist Sanders

Senator Sanders is still running strong. On Good Friday, March 25, 2016, at a rally in Portland, Oregon, a little yellow bird appeared. The over 10,000 fans roared. The bird perched on the podium as he spoke about the importance of education. Sanders smiled. He offered that the bird was a symbolic dove that brought a message of peace: "No more wars," he thundered. It was a cheerful moment. He humanized the campaign as no one had seen in recent years. The little bird stole the show. His supporters stretched the significance to mean that Twitter, which features a bird (what else) as its logo, had endorsed the senator!

If it were not for the dawn of Trumpism, Sanders would have been the undebatable phenom of the 2016 presidential campaigns. He provided the old, feel-good campaign of American presidential primary elections. He appeals to women (with Hillary in the race) and to young people who like what they hear. His speeches make a lot of sense, even if many know that hell will freeze before lobbyists-controlled Congress bows to his policy proposals that the media mostly ignore.

Sanders loses me when he talks about foreign affairs. He always finds a way to circle his answer to highlight that Hillary Clinton voted for the Iraqi War. Mrs. Clinton has paid enough for that 'crime' against liberals: It lost her the primaries against Obama in 2008, and she has apologized profusely… knowing what she knows now. What he lacks in foreign affairs, he makes up on commonsense social issues. Sanders has been hammering on the greed of Wall Street and the scandal that people have to do multiple jobs to make a living.

Sanders appeals to segments of the society that Trump loathes. He reminds them that Trump has led the campaign to delegitimize President Obama because Barack Obama, Sr. was born in Kenya. Now, his own father was born in Poland. To date, he wonders, no one has asked him to produce his birth certificate! On Ms. Sandra Bland, an African American woman who died in Texas police custody after a simple traffic stop, he stated unequivocally that she would still be alive if she were white. True.

If Sanders had run against Barack Obama in the 2012 primaries—and lost, he would have beat Hillary Clinton handsomely in 2016. He made a late entry, and funds started raining late in the game—after Hillary had soaked in the heavy donors and secured the blessings of many superdelegates… purportedly. Still, Sanders has gone on to demolish all the records set by Obama in the numbers that come to his rallies and the amount of money raised from individuals. His campaign is awash with cash, and he is not stopping until the final gong sounds at the Democratic Convention in Philadelphia, or so he says.

Sanders' wife believes in his mission. She is in Alaska campaigning hard for three straight days. It shows that Sanders is pushing not just to win every contest henceforth but also to win big and reduce the margin of Hillary's share of the pledged delegates. Alas, it is a long, long road travel. The Clinton machine looks set to contain the attack of an older Vermont senator of Polish Jewish extraction.

Reality Check on Lying Out Loud

Today Monday, March 28, 2016, marks the first time since I started the journal-like analyses that no primary or caucus will be occupying the news channels. Of course, this does not mean the end of the darling of media cable television: Trump. On the contrary, he is still taking the top of the news. The shooting incident at the entrance into US Congress could not hold the media attention for the day; Trump still dominated the news channels.

In old normal times, Ted Cruz's maneuverings would have topped every newscast, but these are new normal times. It appears that Ted Cruz was not making empty threats when he vowed that Trump would not be the Republican nominee. He (Cruz) had been working the grassroots and poaching delegates supposedly won by Trump to his own column. This is legal, they say, because caucuses and primaries do not really produce party nominees; delegates do, on the Convention floor. The American presidential contest at the party level, at least, is a mean street fight. A relatively decent fighter (as Obama was) only hopes that the emergent opponent would be equally as decent (as was McCain in 2008).

Meanwhile, back from Argentina, Barack Obama catches up with the media spectacle and weighs in with telling the media how to do their job! Something seems wrong with the way media houses portray ongoing election campaigns. In his remarks at the 2016 Donna Toner Prize Ceremony, Obama blamed news media for focusing lightly on individuals and on social media. He urged journalists to ask tough questions of candidates, not just run away with headline-grabbing statements on policies the politicians will never implement.

> The number one question I am getting as I travel around the world or talk to world leaders right now is, what is happening in America -- about our politics. And it's not because around the world people have not seen crazy politics; it is that they understand America is the place where you can't afford completely crazy politics. For some countries where this kind of rhetoric may not have the same ramifications, people expect, they understand, they care about America, the most powerful nation on Earth, functioning effectively, and its government being able to make sound decisions.[22]

President Obama was right about one thing, among many others: If the media continue to serve light news gleaned from Twitter, Facebook, and gazillion web-based news outlets, there will be no incentive to watch television and read newspapers. Once readership and viewership drop, advertising dollars will grow wings and head elsewhere. In the age of smartphones and the fast-changing world of cyberspace, the advice could not have come at a better time.

---

[22] https://www.whitehouse.gov/the-press-office/2016/03/28/remarks-president-2016-toner-prize-ceremony

Without mentioning names, observers knew he was alluding to the Trump phenomenon. For months, the media have given Trump a big pass, never really pinning him down to specifics and always jumping on his many outrageous and outpouring statements. Until recently, no one has stopped Trump to challenge his outlandish claims. Hosts hardly interrupt him on his many phone-ins. Only a Wisconsin-based talk-show host named Charlie Sykes has so far shown the way by interrupting the fast-talking Trump robustly, asking him specific questions, telling him when he is rambling off the questions, and calling him out on obviously childish acts and false statements.

The national cable-news media touted Charlie Sykes as hosting the most popular conservative talk-radio show west of New York's major media market. Actually, he is a big shot in the good state of Wisconsin. He may be as good and as big as bandied around, but many of us out northeast are just hearing about him. Reported as an unabashed #NeverTrump advocate, it was somewhat surprising that Trump showed up in his space by phoning-in on Monday, March 28, just a week before the Wisconsin primaries on Tuesday, April 5. Apparently, no one bothered to tell Trump that he was in an uncharted territory. Charlie Sykes breaks it to him:

> SYKES: "Mr. Trump, before you called into my show, did you know that I'm a #NeverTrump guy?"
> TRUMP: "No, I didn't know that, but I assume you're also an intelligent guy. I know you're an intelligent guy, and you understand what's going on."[23]

---

[23] http://www.politico.com/blogs/2016-gop-primary-live-updates-and-results/2016/03/trump-charlie-sykes-interview-221289

After failing to convince Trump of the need for decorum and civility in presidential campaigns and of the need to offer a simple apology to Mrs. Heidi Cruz, Mr. Sykes delivers a stinger:

> "Is this your standard, that if a supporter of another candidate, not the candidate himself, does something despicable, that it's okay for you, personally, a candidate for president of the United States, to behave in that same way? I mean, I expect that from a 12-year-old bully on the playground."

Obama talked about the "billions of dollars in free media" allocated to Trump and posited that such serious sums should come "with serious accountability, especially when politicians issue unworkable plans or make promises they can't keep." According to *The New York Times*, Trump has received $1.9 billion in free media coverage, more than double the freebies that Hillary Clinton has received ($746 million) and dwarfing Ted Cruz at $313 million.

BREAKING NEWS: Jupiter, Florida police finally did the expected: The police in the Florida town arrested campaign manager Corey Lewandowski and charged him with simple battery, a misdemeanor. This is what keeps American politics sane in a sea of insanity: You can talk, but you do not touch. I knew that Trump's campaign manager would step into a big crap. The last time we saw this campaign manager, he was actually acting like a bouncer, dragging a young lad on a rally floor in Arizona. Lewandowski, 42, was beginning to believe in superpowers. He lied about not touching the young reporter, but there was no evidence of battery.

Mr. Lewandowski may have made a mistake, or he did not know he grabbed someone in trying to protect his principal; however, it is neither kosher to deny the incident outright, nor to deride the reporter. The man is no stranger to such acts. He took a gun into a congressional office building in 1999. He was then a chief of staff to Congressman Bob Ney (R-OH). The police charged him and seized the pistol. He sued to get back his gun and lost.

Campaigning in Janesville, WI, the hometown of Speaker Ryan Paul, Trump made much fuss about the incident, never walking back the derisive comments about Ms. Fields. Again, Trump fueled the misgivings about his attitude towards women. Ms. Michelle Fields, formerly a reporter at the conservative news website *Breitbart*, stands vindicated on her account of the March 8, 2016 incident. This will teach Trump supporters that violence at political events comes with consequences.

Trump's team fired back: "Mr. Lewandowski is absolutely innocent of this charge. He will enter a plea of not guilty and looks forward to his day in court. He is completely confident that he will be exonerated." Trump himself tweeted, "Why aren't people looking at this reporter's earliest statement as to what happened, that is before she found out the episode was on tape?" In what is now a campaign by tweeting, Ms. Fields responded: "My story never changed. Seriously, just stop lying." No matter how the matter resolves, Trump now has an opportunity to pay for someone's legal fees, as he has promised he would do. Hence, in the history of modern American presidential campaigns, the police arraigned a campaign manager for violence.

Reactions from the other candidates were swiftly condemnatory. When asked much later in the evening if Trump should fire Lewandowski, Ted Cruz said, "It shouldn't be complicated that members of the campaign staff should not be physically assaulting the press." Cruz should get a big pass here: He fired his campaign manager for retweeting a fake video purporting that Marco Rubio rubbished a fellow reading the bible.

Kasich agreed that he would have fired Corey Lewandowski. Trump would not fire him, so as not to "ruin his (Lewandowski's) life." He continued his weird ridiculing of Ms. Fields in a futile attempt to try the case in the court of public opinion. "She had a pen in her hand, which Secret Service is not liking because they don't know what it is, whether it's a little bomb." In other words, Ms. Fields was a potential terrorist, and we thought his campaign manager had never met her!

Trump is behaving badly, and the Republican Party knows it. At this point, the party cannot stop the Trump train. If it tries to destroy him forcefully, its electoral fortunes will hit a high wall. No man standing could stop Trump at this point. He knows it, and he is not hiding the fact. The major problem now is how to transition Trump into a serious candidate in the fall. The way things are shaping up, Trump does not look likely to change his ways. No one learns the use of the left hand at an advanced age, and leopards do not change their spots. He is too set in his wacky ways that work well so far to try something different and dicey. On the contrary, his ways could get worse in a possible fall faceoff with Mrs. Hillary Clinton.

26

Trusting Ted; Caging Kasich

It appears that Republicans are rallying around Ted Cruz, the man who, according to Marco Rubio, "is willing to do or say anything to get elected." This morning, Tuesday, March 29, 2016, Governor Scott Walker became the latest in a growing number of governors and former wannabes to endorse Ted Cruz. Walker tweeted, "@TedCruz is the best-positioned candidate to both win the Republican nomination and defeat Hillary Clinton. I'm proud to stand with him." Thus, he joined the long line of Republicans jumping into the gelling movement to derail Trump's train before Cleveland, OH. Mitt Romney, Jeb Bush, and Carly Fiorina had endorsed Ted Cruz.

Senator Cruz is facing a long trip to Cleveland, assuming his ploy cages Kasich. Cruz appears to have an ace he is playing: He has amassed more delegates in New Orleans, although Trump won the state. From what I have heard, it is legit. It is indeed curious that the rules do not appear to be what they say. Sometimes I wonder why candidates bother with primaries when delegates actually count at the convention. *Buy them!*

Trump has his own aces lined up too. First, he strives to get the 1237 delegates before the convention, or close to it. Cruz's citizenship concerns reverberates. As Trump has remarked, "Cruz could be Prime Minister of Canada." He could also be President of the United States! Thirdly, if Trump gets more delegates than Cruz and Kasich "by a lot," he will force the hands of the party or, if that fails, then all bets are off. He may go rogue and float an independent candidacy.

If there was any remaining hope of just charming delegates, CNN town-hall interviews with Anderson Cooper laid them bare. (Obama's admonition is now bearing fruits.) Cooper quickly stopped the candidates at his interviews to clear obvious misrepresentations. He allowed none to ramble on and spew memorized positions and policies. In a segment, Trump offered that he had so far spent about $35 million and that he had taken "the small loans—the people that send $17.50 or $250, even $1,000." Cooper forced Trump to concede that he solicited money, that he got money from individuals through his campaign website. "No, I sell hats and shirts." Then he admitted, "Okay, whatever; it's peanuts, okay? It's peanuts." $9.5 million will surely buy any billionaire trucks of peanuts.

Ted Cruz may have made up his mind never to support Trump, but he was not saying it explicitly. Instead, he predicated his opposition to Trump more on personal considerations: "I'm not in the habit of supporting someone who attacks my wife and my family ... I think nominating Donald Trump would be an absolute train wreck. I think it would hand the general election to Hillary Clinton."

Trump was not relenting: Asked about the photo he retweeted, he blurted, "I thought it was a nice picture of Heidi." It was not, and Trump knew it. This was why Wisconsin-based radio host Charlie Sykes told Trump the other day: "I expect that from a 12-year-old bully on the playground, not somebody who wants the office held by Abraham Lincoln." I believe that the Melania-Heidi photo brouhaha has sealed any hope of Ted Cruz and Donald Trump making up, but you never know with some politicians; they are a terrible tribe of jokers unto themselves.

Trump was the lone holdout on the question of supporting anyone who emerges as the GOP nominee. Party chair Reince Priebus had cajoled him to sign a pledge to support the party nominee. When he was winning, Trump restated the pledge, as did the others. [Rubio was still in the mix then, but he is now asking to keep his delegates intact!] It was no surprise when Trump delivered an emphatic *nyet* on supporting the Republican (GOP) nominee. "No, I don't anymore. ... (Cruz) was essentially saying the same thing."

Governor Kasich offered that the pledge to support the eventual GOP nominee was wrong: "All of us shouldn't even have answered that question." In essence, integrity is not a factor in the jungle of politics. Every man is for himself. The last dude standing wins! Ted Cruz comforts those who are more afraid of his presidency than Trump's brand. The consensus in my circle of pundits is that Trump will be Trump as president: all about himself and making deals that are popular and mostly empty. He will build no walls, and he will not embark on a Don Quixote foreign policy.

Talking about the 2009 shooting at Fort Hood, TX shooting, Ted Crux said it took place in "my home state of Florida." No record showed that Cruz had lived in Florida: Canada, Princeton, NJ, Boston, MA, DC-area, yes! He represents Texas in the US Senate, not Florida. Trust Trump to make mincemeat of such a slight gaffe: "His home state is not Florida. His home state is Texas —it may be Canada. But to the best of my knowledge, it's Texas." Once more, Trump injected the qualification of Cruz to run for the president of United States.

For the mere fact that Donald Trump's opponent is Canadian-born, even if it pans out that Cruz is not qualified to run, everything Trump has said about Obama being born in Kenya has fallen flat on its face. What if Obama was born in Kenya by an American—as was Cruz in Canada? It will be interesting to know what Trump's defense will be when serious interviewers challenge his biased and nasty rants against Obama.

With the pledge to support whomever the party nominates now shredded, Trump may play his third-party option. Kasich probably believes that Trump will be outsmarted and that Cruz may be ruled illegible. This will leave the party with no other choice. If the dust settles, Kasich will beat Hillary. He is the only candidate beating her handsomely in a head-to-head polling of voters. It will be a triumph of decency over vulgarity, a repudiation of just being against something, an enthronement of common sense in governance, and reason restored. Though overlooked often in the media, Kasich has persisted in asking people to believe in him, to vote for him. The likes of Arnold Schwarzenegger believe, but Trump appears unstoppable.

27

Campaign Finance

Paul Ryan sent an email from *<info@nrcc-mail.org>* dated Tue, Mar 29, 2016 3:42 pm. I know how they got my email: the state NJGOP got it from a local candidate I had supported. The email is a good reminder that all 248 Republicans of 345 members of the House of Representatives are up for reelection. Who would have thought that the only games in town are not the presidential primaries! The political buzz about the remaining five candidates from the two parties is so loud not even the Senate contests resonate.

Campaign finance is a serious issue in politics. Governor Gary Johnson said, "My issue with campaign finance is 100 percent disclosure. Wear a suit with patches from your big contributors. Depending on the size of the contribution, that's how big the patch should be." According to Ryan's email, "We are just <u>TWO DAYS</u> away from the biggest federal fundraising deadline of the year—and we're in trouble." Therefore, it solicits funds "to fight alongside me [the Speaker] to protect against the irreparable harm another Nancy Pelosi speakership would bring to our great country."

The demand of the email is direct: "to pitch in before Thursday's FEC deadline" between $25 and $250, or "another amount," which "will be TRIPLE-MATCHED until midnight." The strategy is not bad, but I still wonder what value one gets from tossing in all that money into the war chest of politicians. There must be a better way of making campaigns cheaper.

Money drives elections in America, a vast land. To excite voters, politicians must reach the grassroots in diverse places from beyond Ponce, Puerto Rico to Anchorage, Alaska, and from Mattawamkeag, Maine to Honolulu, Hawaii, and beyond. It is not an easy feat to accomplish. I doubt that any candidate has ever visited all these places. In seven years, President Obama is yet to visit all 50 states… forget the outlying US Virgin Islands on the Atlantic Ocean and Guam in the South Pacific. Campaigning for office is capital-intensive. It cost both Obama and Romney over one billion dollars each to execute the 2012 presidential election. Imagine that Trump paid for all the free publicity he is getting, currently estimated to be worth two billion dollars, and the primaries are still on the halfway mark.

The role of money in US politics is becoming unsustainable. In his 2010 state-of-the-union address, Obama condemned Supreme Court ruling on campaign finance, to the visible discomfort of Justice Samuel A. Alito, Jr., who muffled inappropriately—if not rudely, "Not true." As a senator, Obama had voted down the elevation of Alito, so he probably got one back! What Obama said about Citizens United v. Federal Election Commission, which was decided the week before, made sense:

"With all due deference to separation of powers, last week the Supreme Court reversed a century of law that, I believe, will open the floodgates for special interests, including foreign corporations, to spend without limit in our elections. I don't think American elections should be bankrolled by America's most powerful interests or, worse, by foreign entities. They should be decided by the American people. And I urge Democrats and Republicans to pass a bill that helps correct some of these problems."

Obama's founded fear of money hijacking our democracy has not quite panned out. On the contrary, both Trump and Sanders, as with Obama before them, have shown that "the American people" will buy into anyone's good vision if properly presented, sufficiently sugared or not. Obama presented a rosy picture, a future where neither race nor religion will feature in the political discourse. He straddles both sides of the issue —black and white, Christianity and Islam. Americans believed Obama and ignored Bill Clinton's post-Iowa "fairytale" and South Carolina "myth and mugging" mockery. Eight years later, it is Trump's turn to spin!

Trump talks sense to Tommy Tawms and to those that do not like the other candidates. Sanders, on the other hand, largely preaches unattainable social policies that do not favor big businesses. They got their messages across without any other "powerful interest" but people power. Hillary Clinton stayed on the old and paved path of pay-to-play politics and power peddling. She welcomes millionaires and superstars from New York's Wall Street and Los Angeles' Hollywood and anywhere in-between.

Often, it is better to let events unfold; abridging them may yield unintended consequences and needless collateral damages. In a decent democracy, the people will eventually correct sticky anomalies in the system. Corrections of political problems may take some years. Someone at some point will stand and tell the people the truth, which rubs the minority with high stakes the wrong way. Still, the majority always prevails at last. That is the essence of democracy: the majority gets its way after everyone has had his or her say. No matter the issue, from abortion to ageism, from drugs to death penalty, and from jails to jobs, democracy corrects them.

The likes of Rachael Maddow help to advance the discussions that lead to corrections. I have known of Dr. Maddow since Keith Olbermann, the ace liberal political commentator. She eased me out of the funk of losing Keith on MSNBC. Everyone likes Rachael. She is a very nice person, and that is saying a whole lot. I like her friendly simple style and the seriousness of her poignant presentations. In this election cycle, she got her tenure as the 'professor of *poofology*'!

On Tuesday, March 29, she revisited the "DC Madam" scandal. Deborah Jeane Palfrey passed in 2008, but the records of escort agency services still exist. Her attorney Montgomery Blair Sibley had been threatening to release the records, whether the US Supreme Court agrees or disagrees, and to change the direction of the presidential elections. The way *TRMS* handled the story tonight is typical of Maddow's approach: A thorough and light-hearted foray into related history, an ease-up on the issue at stake, and everyone is ready to ride with her on a journey of discovery.

28

Takedown Trump

Barry Goldwater notably said, "Extremism in the defense of liberty is no vice. And moderation in the pursuit of justice is no virtue." However, rudeness is no virtue, neither is crudeness—not in the defense of liberty, nor in the pursuit of justice. Rudeness is a sign that something is wrong with an otherwise normal person. Albeit not specifically listed as a symptom of narcissism, rudeness is definitely a lack of empathy and an acute inclination to exploit others by degrading them—which are some of the set symptoms of narcissistic personality disorder.

I agree with the movie character M Gustave[24] played by Ralph Fiennes in Wes Anderson's thrilling movie *The Grand Budapest Hotel.*

> Rudeness is merely the expression of fear. People fear they won't get what they want. The most dreadful and unattractive person only needs to be loved, and they will open up like a flower.

---

[24] A convoluted concierge in the 2014 movies about a popular 1930s European hotel and ski resort in Budapest played by Ralph Fiennes.

Mr. Donald Trump's insidious invectives are no longer news; they are now a major part of the prevailing political discourse. The trail of Trump's tirades is long. Some are easy to dismiss; others are profound. Some outbursts are unnecessary and unprovoked; others are, as he would put it, counterpunches. Many of his rude remarks flow from the bottom of juvenile badmouthing and spiteful belittling. In the process, he has made lifelong enemies for himself. His victims are many.

I first noticed his gutter snipping when he went into the Tabloid sewer with Rosie O'Donnell. He later picked the Birther's cause and went after President Obama as if he knew a whole lot more than the rest of us: He did not; he knew a lot less—he was designing an alternate universe and hoping that its planets harbor different folks with different measures for falsehood. His fantasies could not just be about hugging the mic and staying in the news; it must be something deeper that only is a good shrink could diagnose. Alarmingly, Trump's ways work for him, and they work well so far in the 2016 presidential primaries!

Trump doubled down on Governor Rick Perry (R-TX), relegated him to the kid's table debates and ran out him out of the race. His low-energy blow on Jeb Bush was so mean it actually stuck. Jeb had no response except to take the high road vowing that Trump could not "insult his way to the White House." For far too long, Senator Ted Cruz enjoyed the exchanges from the shadows, hoping to pick up the pieces whenever the American people felt that they had heard enough. This was before Trump descended on Cruz with the harsh "Lyin' Ted" epithet.

Ben Carson had little to say to Trump. Come high water or hurricane, he stayed on bashing Obama when he got the chance. No one takes such hits as Carson took from Trump without firing back with full force. He took it all in strides; he only once questioned Trump's faith and later offered lamely that Trump has two sides to his character. It was hard to decode from Carson's startling dullard demeanor whether he was referring to a bad medical disorder or shining a light on hidden qualities of Trump that only those closest to him knew.

Senator Lindsey Graham found out the hard way that tumbling with Trump is akin to playing with our feathered friends—fowls: you leave with foul hands. As an old proverb has it, he who wrestles with the gorilla must sport a sand-stained back. To get even, Trump not only dissed Graham for asking him for money, he also publicized his cell phone number on national television! Graham was a good sport: he made a little political gain by smashing the phone with a golf club. What no one said in the Trump-obsessed media was that smashing a cell phone does not the phone numbers erase!

Governor Bobby Jindal (R-LA) decided early to hit back at Trump and damn the consequences. When Trump threw his usual dismissive Twitter jive that "Jindal did not make the [big boys'] debate stage and therefore I have never met him...," Jindal shot back and repeated the same rebuttal on television later:

> @realdonaldtrump We have met. You wrote a check. A fool & his money are soon parted. A fool & his dad's money are parted sooner.
>
> 3:13 PM - 10 Sep 2015

Ouch!

Trump ignored Jindal thenceforth. It made sense: The governor was gathering no traction in the polls. It is a waste of time to beat up a sinking enemy; you may instead offer him a straw he could grab and get out. Trump stayed on those who are too close for comfort. He did not spare Chris Christie, who was closer to him and knew a lot about his deals in New Jersey. On the sensitive Bridgegate scandal, which was still under scrutiny by federal attorneys, Trump passed his verdict from the debate podium and prejudged Christie guilty.

Christie got it wrong; he had fired the first salvo! After Trump delivered his wish for "total and complete" ban of all Muslim entering the United States, Christie said of the "ridiculous position":

> This is the kind of thing that people say when they have no experience and don't know what they're talking about. We do not need to endorse that type of activity, nor should we.

That was all Trump needed to come out with big guns in both hands and shooting from the hips. He had a menu of bullets, from Christie's controversial hugging of Obama during Hurricane Sandy in 2012, through the downgrading of New Jersey's credit under Christie to the simmering Bridgegate. The comments from Christie hurt Trump, and he said so at a rally somewhere in South Carolina: "I've been nice to Christie, but he really hit me today. He's a friend of mine, but he's not doing well in the polls. And he really, really hit me today."

Having prepared the audience, as if to justify his mantra of only counter-punching, of not insulting until insulted, he delivered on all fronts by saying in parts:

So, Chris, who is a friend of mine, he hit me hard, and I said I got to hit him at least once. So I won't do this a lot, but, look, here's the story: The George Washington Bridge. He knew about. How do you have breakfast with people every day of your lives and not know? They're closing up the largest bridge in the world—the biggest in the United States—traffic flowing during rush hour. People couldn't get across for six, seven hours. Ambulances. Fire trucks.

They're with him all the time, the people that did it. They never said, 'Hey, boss, uh, we're closing up the George Washington Bridge.' No, they never said that, they're talking about the weather? Right?! He knew about it. He totally knew about it. He's got a very friendly group of people over there."

Trump was right: There was no way a governor would not know of such a massive shutdown of the busiest bridge in USA. The scandal has hurt Christie, and the case is only just beginning to unfold. Whatever lifeline Christie was holding out disappeared on that day. It was Christie's Pearl Harbor and Waterloo on that December 7, 2015. Trump the "chaos candidate" (according to Christie) found a way to steal the spotlight and beat back the jab from Jersey.

Trump perches on pickles, addressing issues casually and shamelessly, be they simple or sacred. Imagine what he said about Carly Fiorina in a *Rolling Stone* interview of September 2015: "Look at that face! Would anyone vote for that? Can you imagine that, the face of our next president?!" That hurt, but Carly took it in calmly when it came up at a *CNN* debate: "I think women all over this country heard very clearly what Mr. Trump said." Trump walked it back. No apologies!

What was the birther movement all about again? Assuming Obama was born in, say, Kitengela, Kenya, by an American mother from Kansas, white or black: what difference does it make? Assuming Barack Obama was a Muslim, an adherent of a faith embraced by his grandfather, what difference does it make? Trump could have made an issue of the eligibility of being born outside USA, as done lamely with Cruz, not question the citizenship of Obama long after his swearing in as president. Oh, I forgot that Kenya is not Canada, and Cuban Cruz is not Kenyan Obama. Racism is often so innate the racist does not know he has the disease!

Here is a man who, long after his bizarre birther buffoonery burned in a blaze of lies, still will not say that Obama is a valid president. How could such a person, who disrespects an office he aspires to occupy, succeed in the quest? Trump's bias is laid bare by his embrace of Cruz 's candidacy in the primaries; his tepid threats to sue was a joke. He did not send investigators to Canada. Compare with his vociferous anti-Obama campaign, lying about sending people to Hawaii and about unearthing unbelievable evidence about nothing.

Trump surely cannot take as much as he gives: Three decades after Graydon Carter poked him for fun, he is yet to get over the "short-fingered vulgarian" quip. Days after Marco Rubio left the primaries stage, Trump is yet to live down the size of his anatomical extremities. In the now infamous interview with *Washington Post* on Monday, March 21, 2016, Trump defended again the enduring counterpunch by Marco Rubio to his many "Little Marco" punches. Trump had a ready answer for anyone wondering why he kept bringing up the issue:

"I don't want people to go around thinking that I have a problem." Asked if talking about his private part in public debates was presidential, Trump talked about what must have been eating him up from the inside:

> I don't know if it was presidential, honestly, whether it is or not. He [Rubio] said, 'Donald Trump has small hands and therefore he has small something else.' I didn't say that. And all I did is when he failed, when he was failing, when he was, when Christie made him look bad, I gave him the– a little recap and I said, and I said, and I had this big strong powerful hand ready to grab him, because I thought he was going to faint. And everybody took it fine. Whether it was presidential or not I can't tell you. I can just say that what he said was a lie. And everybody, they wanted to do stories on my hands; after I said that, they never did. And then I held up the hand, I showed people the hand. You know, when I've got a big audience. So yeah, I think it's not a question of presidential ....[25]

Trump was taking the little jibes so seriously. What about those he had punched so badly into pulps, should they coil up and hide? I believe that given a legal situation of, say, self-defense, he could have grabbed Rubio by the neck just to show he has strong hands. Recall the incident in Ohio, when a protester tried to jump up the stage. Trump might have been scared, but he clenched those hands ready to throw a punch and show what strong hands he has. It took secret service agents to restrain Trump, not necessarily to safeguard him from the distressed denizen.

---

[25] https://www.washingtonpost.com/blogs/post-partisan/wp/2016/03/21/a-transcript-of-donald-trumps-meeting-with-the-washington-post-editorial-board/

On Wednesday, March 30, in a town hall meeting with Chris Matthews on MSNBC's *Hardball*, Trump made a statement that marked the clear beginning of Trump's takedown by both fellow Republicans and Democrats. The statements bothered on not taking 'nuking Europe' off the table and punishing women for having abortions. In a heated but civil exchange, Chris Matthews stayed on Trump like no other TV host, never allowing him to dodge the relevant questions and never allowing him to dictate the direction of the interview.

The approach was in line with what Obama had requested in his speech on Monday. CNN's Anderson Cooper had also towed the same line. Before then, radio host Charles Sykes of Wisconsin had broken the mold of padded-glove pugilism. NBC's Chuck Todd had attempted to checkmate Trump when he claimed that his alleged attacker at a political rally had connections with ISIS. Chris Wallace also tried to pooh-pooh Trump's claims at the Fox debate. Of course, Megyn Kelly wears the scars from presenting uncomfortable facts to Trump.

Mr. Trump had no hiding place once Matthews posed probing queries about abortions. Just mouthing, "I am pro-life," was not enough; more was required. Trump exposed his ignorance of the pro-life platform by promising "some form of punishment" for a woman having an abortion. Did he know what he was saying? He did not flinch: he could handle truth and untruth *pari passu*. Here is the man who in one breathe loves protesters and pleads, "Don't hurt the protesters"; in another, he is encouraging his listeners to punch them! *"Lying out loud"* has a pictorial depiction in Trump.

29

Clinton Coal

Hillary Clinton said today, Thursday, March 31, 2016, "I am so sick. I am so sick of the Sanders campaign lying about me. I'm sick of it." She made the statement with all the vocal vigor she could muster in response to a simple request by a climate-change activist: Did she accept money from the fossil fuel industry? Senator Sanders had early alleged that she did indeed accept "millions of dollars" from the industry. The answer is simple: Yes. Clinton campaign has accepted donations but, according to her, "I do not have that kind of money from people who work for fossil fuel companies."

No one really cares how much money Hillary has received, forget that Sanders mentions "millions," which is obviously incorrect. The question was whether she accepted money that came from the fossil fuel folks. She did indeed; maybe not directly from the companies, but definitely from lobbyists who work as agents of the companies concerned. American politicians get money from sundry sources; none is without some strings attached, and none is beyond constructive criticisms.

Mrs. Clinton may not "have that kind of money from people who work for fossil fuel companies," but it is difficult to defend that money is not coming from a particular industry for both candidates. It is true that Sanders does not take money from industries and Wall Street, but people who work in the industries contribute money to both campaigns, though only Sanders signed the Greenpeace pledge not to take money from fossil fuel industries. The bottom line is that as long as the donations are legitimate, it is wrong to castigate another candidate for accepting donations. These wily lobbyists also contribute to the election campaigns of lawmakers and state/city executives—governors and mayors

It is not the first time that the former first lady expressed being "sick and tired." In 2003, the then Senator Clinton rebuked President George W. Bush:

> I'm sick and tired of people who say that if you debate and disagree with this administration, somehow you're not patriotic. We need to stand up and say we're Americans, and we have the right to debate and disagree with any administration.

She was right. Compared with what Republicans did and do to Barack Obama's administration, Mrs. Clinton's was child play. In addition, she had voted for the Iraqi War, a vote that predominantly cost her the DNC nomination in 2008. The vote, for which she has apologized profusely, still dogs her in 2016.

Senator Sanders is also insincere in impeaching the amount of money paid in private speaking fees to Mrs. Clinton. As Sanders spoke around the country, his supporters contribute millions to hear him. If these fees are not speaking fees, they are definitely not tithes!

In March alone, Sanders raked in a whopping $44 million. That is a lot of money to haul in from public speeches. Speaking in South Bronx today, Sanders doubled down on the issue of campaign contributions: "Hillary owes us an apology. We are not lying; we are telling the truth." Sanders can afford not to take money from big corporations; he is doing just fine with online contributions. Reports show that he has collected much more money than Obama's record-breaking hauls from money mining on the Internet. Sanders has upped the ante, so it is easy for him to stand on a podium and point a finger at Mrs. Clinton for raking in from the usual source of campaign funding—lobbyists.

Clinton has a new Shame-on-you-Barack-Obama moment on the last day of March in Purchase, New York. Senator Bernie Sanders has been hitting her hard lately with every tool in his garage. He complains about her reluctantly agreeing to debate him, when she said the same of Obama in 2008. He also complains of Hillary prying superdelegates. Sanders has an eye on donors sending in more millions of dollars on the momentum of his Alaska, Hawaii, and Washington sweep with large intimidating numbers in the 70 percentiles.

It is ironic that Hillary complains about taking money from lobbyists of fossil fuel industry—which is not a crime. In 2008, she criticized Obama for accepting only $200,000 from "executives and employees" of the same oil industry. The ad, which is still available on Youtube.com, claimed, "It's been against the law for 100 years" to take money from oil companies.

Change is good, but raising money from any business entity or private citizen is legal. To make it look as it Hillary is committing a crime is dubious and misleading. In politics, people of Sanders' stature should tell the truth. On the other hand, pointing out the sources of Clinton campaign funds is not a crime. Mrs. Clinton got it wrong by flaring up. Opponents can use issues that resonate to dominate the airwaves.

The 2016 season has been about Trump taking over the airwaves and information superhighway (via Twitter). How he achieves the feat is impeachable, but it is the nature of politics to prowl along the edges of social norms. Often, a backlash occurs; politicians recoil. Life goes on. Trump has so far weathered the storms from his outrageous statements without a major retreat. It is understandable that Sanders intentionally agitates Clinton, but psychological offensive is a part of the war without bloodshed.

However, Hillary is a vetted veteran of political campaigns; she has been involved all her adult life. She should know that such sidebar talks do not make an election make. Motivating voters to go to the polls makes more difference. She should have ignored Sanders and taken the high road. It is true that Sanders campaign is out to get her, for obvious reasons that are principally political, but to posit that her opponent is spreading lies about her is a lie.

30

Manifest Mendacities

The level of lying has risen to such a state that a super PAC called "New Day for America"—said to be supporting Governor Kasich (R-OH), released one of the wackiest television attack ads of the season so far. Probably hoping to cut down the surge of Senator Ted Cruz in the Wisconsin April 5 primaries, the political action group hatched a hard-hitting attack ad. Ironically, attacking Cruz at a time that taking down Trump should be the focus may shore up the sagging statistics for Trump who, in some polls, trails Ted Cruz by double digits.

Proverbs 19:5 states: "A false witness shall not be unpunished, and he that speaketh lies shall not escape." It happened for Ted Cruz; he could not escape his lies. In a made-for-television political advertisement released today Thursday, March 31, a recitation of lies allegedly told by Ted Cruz follows his awkwardly growing nose as in the story of Pinocchio. Instead of just growing out, in this case, the nose grows so long it wraps around the senator's neck three times. Labelled "Nose," the 30-second ad reads:

"Many just call him, 'Lyin' Ted.' Lied about Ben Carson to steal a win in Iowa. Lies about being the best for the GOP, when polls show he can't even beat Hillary Clinton. His TV ad about John Kasich? Lie. Stations had pulled it off the air. If Ted Cruz's mouth is moving, he's lying."

Kasich reportedly apologized for the attack ad… wait a minute: the ad clearly indicated that it was "not authorized by any candidate or candidate's committee." The purported mea culpa is yet another political ploy, an obvious copout after catching a grown man holding the missing cookie from a cookie jar. Why would a super PAC shell out half a million dollars without first clearing with the beneficiary? The only thing that connected Kasich is the half-truth that the ad tells: "Only Kasich can beat Hillary." Well, some polls show that Senator Sanders is also beating Hillary Clinton in a match up, and Sanders is beating Kasich.

The attack ad is an ill-advised gamble. Governor John Kasich is running a hopeless fourth in a field of three remaining Republican candidates; Rubio still has more delegates than Kasich. If the plot is to keep Trump from nailing 1237 delegates, the only candidate who could do it in Wisconsin is Ted Cruz. Crippling Cruz in such a fight will only prop up Trump's drop this week. It is not likely that Cruz's camp will swallow the hurt and let the ad ride. Therefore, if Trump pulls out a win in Wisconsin next Tuesday, blame the takedown-Ted tactics from Kasich's camp. Although he has vowed not to consider being vice presidential candidate, Kasich will make a terrible deputy. His highest hooray is really winning his state of Ohio. His case is closed.

It is a month-end of mischiefs, minor mea culpas, and accusations of inaccuracies. The most striking event is the involvement of Kasich's camp in the attack ads. This comes from the same Kasich who on Friday, March 11 swore that "wallowing in the mud with Donald is not what I think is a successful strategy." Why wallow with Ted Cruz in the mud?

On the other hand, Ted Cruz cannot complain: He has thrown so many stones; he deserves a few hits. Aside from insulting his congressional majority leader Mitch McConnell on the sacred floor of the Senate, Cruz has a knack for telling tales about his elders. Hear him dig into Biden on Thursday, June 3, 2015, days after the vice president lost his son Beau to cancer:

> "Vice President Joe Biden. You know the nice thing? You don't need a punch line. I promise you, it works. The next party you're at, just walk up to someone, say 'Vice President Joe Biden,' and just close your mouth. They will crack up laughing."

Joseph "Beau" Biden III, who died on Saturday, May 30, 2015 at 46, was to be buried the day after Cruz's cruel comment! Cruz considered no apology until social and other media shamed him. He wrote an apology on Facebook: "It was a mistake to use an old joke about Joe Biden during his time of grief, and I sincerely apologize. The loss of his son is heartbreaking and tragic, and our prayers are very much with the Vice President and his family." It was indeed an overused "old joke" that was unamusing. He had used it repeatedly in his campaign stump speeches. It was as if he was running to replace Joe Biden as the US vice president.

Trust Vice President Joe Biden: he knows how to get back at the wise and fools alike. Appearing at the Gridiron Dinner (where politicians poke fun freely at each other) on Saturday, March 5, 2016, he maturely took Ted Cruz to the cleaners with one of the best jokes about the junior senator from Texas... before Senator Lindsey Graham took the tacos. Here is Biden on Cruz:

> Ted Cruz? An inspiration to every kid in America who worries that he'll never be able to run for president because nobody likes him. He's running. And look, I told Barack [Obama], if you really, really want to remake the Supreme Court, nominate Cruz. Before you know it, you'll have eight vacancies.

Ouch!

Ted Cruz is definitely a likeable person. He just makes it too easy for people not to like him once he opens his mouth. He takes himself too seriously. He is too rigid in his beliefs as if knowledge stopped the day he left law school. His jokes are not funny, when told by him; they sound like tales from the lab of Mary Shelley's *Victor Frankenstein*.

31

A Month of Mischiefs

I am in Atlantic City, New Jersey, a city facing the brunt of economic crises that the city managers have brought on the citizens. AC is a rich-man-poor-man showcase. In 1989, I saw poverty beneath the glittering glass casinos and on the boardwalks. It was odd. I told my host that such crass capitalism could not sustain. It took three decades, many more years than I had anticipated. This place is going down.

Looking out of my hotel room in the Sheraton at the Convention Center, I see few tourists walking the neat streets. Workers wearing gloomy faces occasionally stream in and out of near-empty eateries and half-empty halls. The parking places are eerily empty. The Center that used to be a beehive of events looks dingy. It is no wonder that the State of New Jersey under Governor Christie is taking over the city management. The state might as well take over the empty shell of an unholy cow that made cash; it has raked in enough dough to own the shell of a former trendy town. At Six Flags, you get great rides, which is why people go here; AC without a thriving casino culture is comatose.

With the whistling wind and cold weather, I have no interest in walking down to the Atlantic Boardwalk, let alone trying to romance Lady Luck with the glitzy, gaming slot machines. These thieving devices, formerly called 'one-armed bandits,' I now call *'click criminals'*! I am in no mood to party either, and I do not subscribe to long hospitality-room hangouts. I retire to my room with a great view of the city to watch some television.

The level of lying and denials in the continuing primary elections has reached a new height. Television programs and websites dedicate time to fact-check the offerings of all remaining candidates, especially Trump. The development is logical and welcome in an age of all-comer political punditry and social-media activism, where a casual commentary soon becomes news. It is not only that lies fly in the face of obvious truths, it is troubling that politicians call out each other on lies. Calling candidates "liars" implicitly and explicitly has become acceptable.

Commentators gloss over John Kasich, Ted Cruz, and Donald Trump reneging on their public pledge to support the party's eventual nominee. The truth is that every political party has stable rules of engagement. Everyone is welcome to work within the set rules, navigate the nuances as deftly as possible, and strive to emerge a victor. One person will win; others will lose. The winner becomes the leader for a prescribed period. The question of the vanquished supporting the victor needs not arise because injecting indiscipline into any political formation is a recipe for electoral misfortune. Alas, these are not normal primary elections; something in the air does not smell good for the Republicans.

Lying has become so pervasive in politics. "The Mendacity Index"[26] now measures on a scale of 1 and 5 which president told the biggest lies. If you think Bill Clinton (of draft-dodging, not-inhaling fame) ranks tops for the Lewinsky affair, think again. Reagan (arms-for-hostages, Iran Contra) told lies that are more serious at 3.3 to Clinton's 3.1. George W Bush took the trophy home at 3.6 with weapons of mass destruction that existed only in VP Dick Cheney's mind and other sundry fibs. GW scored more than his father, George H. Bush ("read my lips"), at 3.2.

It is a part of the new culture of *lying out loud* that people pledge to support someone and then renege. That is emotional immaturity, a character defect arising from innate inability to give honest answers to simple questions. We must also add *Jebism*: answering a simple question wrongly. At the rosy start of his campaign, a *Fox News* moderator asked Jeb Bush if knowing what he knew now, would he have gone to war in Iraq? Simple question, simple answer; nothing could be simpler. How many men worldwide would say, and pass a lie detector test, that knowing what they know now they would have married the same woman and in the same way as they did years ago? That is how basic the answer is: NO! Of course, a philosopher will add that hindsight is 20/20, and a politician could say that he *might* not. Whether it was a success or a mistake, the answer to the question about Iraq could not be *YES!* People died. Destruction was deep and vast. Now, we have ISIS, or ISIL—as President Obama prefers to call the group.

---

[26] Washington Monthly, September 2003

The Dawn of Trump

The Republican Party leadership must have seen the coming of a Donald Trump. After the 2012 loss, a half-hearted attempt to recruit moderating minorities failed. Dumping its Black chair, Michael Steele, after winning back the House, raised no eyebrows because Blacks see no future in the party; the Democratic Party is their base. The Republicans allowed the Tea Party to hijack the party in some constituencies. The Tea Party elevated such hotheaded politicians as Ted Cruz. In a primary election in Virginia, the Tea drive evicted then House majority leader Eric Cantor, a Jew. The tea of a party within a party slowly sipped into the Republican body politics, but many tea partiers wanted more. Problems popped up: political correctness and funding. Trump provided solutions: brash talk and an apparent money-not-an-issue plot. The mass media swallowed Trump's bait. The rest is history in the making.

The strident anti-Obama stance was a bad move. Mitch McConnell publicly stated that making Obama a one-term presidency was his life's political ambition. He failed, but he became the Senate majority leader. In the quest to demonize Obama, and for fear of losing their grip on grassroots faithful, the party bosses ignored many levelheaded Republicans. They drove African Americans and other hyphenated Americans farther away. In the process, Republicans lost a great number of new immigrants from Africa, Asia, and Europe, who harbor the values that the party preaches, not the tax-and-spend Democratic position. The party certainly has a serious minority-insensitive problem—not just a demographic minority but also economic minority.

It is ironic that the have-nots of the Republican Party (the socioeconomic minority), have found a leader in a rich capitalist from New York City, NY of all places. If Bernie Sanders had the deep pockets, moderated his socialist agenda, defended the right to own bazookas and Kalashnikovs, and other core conservative causes, he too could have carried the group. Trump is strong on these issues. The Republicans appear to be harnessing some anti-Trump momentum only because Ted Cruz has emerged as its major beneficiary. Cruz is a Tea Party loyalist. He is a conservative hawk. He is an evangelical believer on the fringes of Christian fundamentalism. Trump is not like Ted Cruz; he is not a person of faith, and he has few credible conservative credentials. Those who voted for Trump earlier did not take a closer look at Cruz, his unresolved Canadian connection aside.

Denegrofication **of the White House**

Larry Wilmore is right: Republicans frantically want to replace Obama with their own. Nothing wrong with that; it comes with the territory. However, when they ignore the birthplace of Cruz, it smacks of a double standard, if not blatant racism. Assuming a white or black American mother gave birth to Obama in Kenya; so what? Barack Obama subscribed to the religion of his grandfather, which his own father did not quite follow. Assuming Obama went to a madrasa in Indonesia while over there with his mother as a child; so what? Obama went to the church of Rev Jeremiah Wright, who within his constitutional First Amendment rights said extreme stuff against America; have they read Trump put down the same country in *"Crippled America"*?

Ted Cruz, if nominated, comes with a baggage. He has cozied up to fundamentalist preachers who call for the killing of gays. For months, he nodded smugly to everything that Donald Trump spewed against fellow Latinos of Mexican extraction, Muslims, and other minorities, including the disabled. Reportedly, Calgary-born Canadian-Cuban Cruz was still a Canadian citizen when he got to the Senate; he dropped it on getting ready to race for the White House. This same man sat back, watched, and enjoyed the demonizing of Obama for supposedly being born in a phantom city in Kenya! This is the height of hypocrisy.

At a campaign rally out west in Seattle, Sanders revealed that his father was not born in America; he was born in Poland—as Barack Obama's father was born in Kenya. Why has no one queried Sanders' citizenship? "No one had asked to see my birth certificate." What the senator forgot to add was that no one has queried his religion either, what synagogue he has visited, or what the rabbis said or did not say. No one has made a point of his Jewishness either.

Who has seen Donald Trump in a church of any known denomination? The only question that arose during the conference of American Israel Public Affairs Committee (AIPC-2016) was his pro-Israel credentials. Mr. Trump cited his Jewish connections. Israel may be a Jewish state, but not every Israeli is a Jew, and not every Jew is an Israeli. He offered that his son-in-law Jared Kushner is Jewish and "My daughter Ivanka is about to have a beautiful Jewish baby." His pledge to "move the American embassy to the eternal capital of the Jewish people, Jerusalem" has received no serious scrutiny.

Misreading the Mood

Tommy Tawms consider immigration, especially of people who do not look like them, to be security and socioeconomic risks to their way of life, their jobs, and their entitlements. The influx of Democratic Tawms to the Republicans did not go as expected. They found similar problems in GOP, without Obama. Obviously, it must be something else farther from the non-White man in the White House that Blacks built.

One of the early and most significant revolts was the takedown of House majority leader Eric Cantor by a new-to-politics, local professor named Dave Brat. The party still did not get the memo: this was not a stroke of bad luck for Mr. Cantor but a revolt within its ranks. The Tea Party platform had not only hardened the core of the old Republican Party, the influx of disaffected Democrats introduced another dimension. To make matters worse, the Republican Party legislators sided with Obama on the Pacific trade pact as well as gave away the Iran deal. In the process, the Republicans created a base that is detached from the leadership, a base waiting for a leader who *understands* them and will do what they want.

Enter Trump. He may not believe everything that he is saying. Sincerely speaking, he cannot deliver them. Yet, he talks casually about these issues and Tawms like what they hear: better trade deals with China and Japan; bringing back jobs; walling off Mexico; making imports more expensive; and no talks about American exports! His audience understands and likes his no-PC language. It is harsh, but Trumpites are in no mood for fancy frills. They want firm facts. Trump delivers.

CLINTON & SANDERS

Clinton has a new *Shame-on-you-Barack-Obama* moment on this last day of March in Purchase, New York. Senator Bernie Sanders has been hitting her hard with every tool in his garage. He has called her out for dragging on more debate dates when, in 2008, she called out Obama for not debating and saying that "maybe he prefers to give speeches than to have to answer questions." Sanders also snoops at her superdelegates, rakes in millions more on the momentum of Alaska, Hawaii, and Washington sweep with large intimidating numbers in the 70 percentiles (but with a sharing of delegates), and raves about her taking money from fossil fuel industry—which is not a crime.

Sanders can afford not to take money from big corporations; he is doing well. He is doing much more in donations than Obama's record-breaking hauls from the mines of the Internet. Sanders has upped the ante, so it is easy for him to stand on a podium and point a finger at Hillary for raking in from the usual sources of political campaign funding—businesses and individuals regardless of their legitimate sources of income.

Change is good, but it is not against the law to raise money from the industries. To make it look as if Hillary Clinton has committed a crime is dubious and misleading. In politics, people of Bernie Sanders' stature should tell the truth, and that is the main attraction of the young ones, the millennials, who flock to his rallies. They trust his grandfatherly tales and appreciate the decent way he tells them. Attacking Mrs. Clinton the way he is doing will only lead to a Gore-Bush moment or, more appropriately, a Lazio-Clinton moment.

People did not quite get why Al Gore invaded the space of George Bush in a Y2K presidential debate. It was a turnoff that portrayed the then VP as aggressive. Bush beat him in Tennessee, Gore's state, and won the presidency.

When Senator Moynihan passed, the Democrats recruited a new New Yorker to take the seat. So on September 13, 2000, Congressman Rick Lazio left his debating podium and walked over menacingly to an overwhelmed Mrs. Clinton, shoving a paper to her face and waging his finger. I recall Lazio saying afterwards that it was "sexist" and "double standard" to expect that a man should not make his point strongly because the other person was a woman. "I don't think people in the Senate worry about whether you're a man or a woman," especially one who was aspiring to grace the sacrosanct US Senate Chamber. Well, senators do not elect senators; the people of a state do. By the time many pundits and comedians finished lampooning the "sexist bullying," Lazio was cooked. Hillary Clinton won by double digits.

Senator Sanders' campaign could cross that line in the coming days. His pointing out the sources of Clinton campaign contributions is not a crime. Sourcing of funds from whomever will cough up contributions is legitimate. On the other hand, Mrs. Clinton got it wrong by flaring up. Opponents use whatever issue resonates with voters to dominate the airwaves, embellished or not. The 2016 season has been about Mr. Trump taking over the radio airwaves, television cables, and the information superhighway (via Twitter) with numerous bloated bandying of blames—right or wrong.

It is understandable that the emergence of the Brooklyn-born Jewish, socialist senator from Vermont flusters Hillary, but she is an old political powerhouse. She sure knows that such talks come with the territory. It is okay that Sanders' campaign wants to get her out of its path to the Democratic nomination by stretching the truth, but to posit that her opponent is spreading lies about her is not quite the whole truth.

As the March of mendacities meanders off the high season of primaries, the candidates should be acting presidential and less like schoolyard bullies. Unfortunately, these events are no ordinary primaries. Senator Sanders has raked in $44 million in March, and many more contributors are lining up to ensure that he continues to chip away at Mrs. Clinton's numbers and possibly force an open convention. A big mistake!

On the other side, no one knows what Trump will do next. He could surprise America and call it quits ... if the Republican Party plays by skewed rules. That would be his bet; running as a third-party candidate will only spoil the soup. If Republicans roll over and hand over the nomination ticket to Trump, and Hillary Clinton wins the Democratic ticket, then all bets are off. Forget the current polls: things will toughen up a bit. Something is driving Trump; he alone knows his true intentions and the spirits that possess all his supporters, the Tommy Tawms, who will not desert him as long as the aroma of their promised paradise hangs in the air. Therefore, the Republican plot to stop Trump should channel to stopping what produced and propelled him, for the fragrance of fart foretells the flavor of feces.

Epilogue

March Madness happened. The popular USA college basketball tournaments featured on the television for aficionados to enjoy. Dedicated fans followed the battles of elite university basketball teams religiously. I saw segments, but I did not quite follow the competitions. Mid-March, Barack Obama filled out his usual, bracket presidential predictions called *"Baracketology."* An avid basketball fan and player, we will miss the sports-loving president. I do not know Hillary Clinton to be into any sports, besides supporting the Cubs of her native Chicago. Donald Trump is interested if it makes him money, such as golfing on his private courses, and pro-boxing in his then casinos with Donald (Don) King as the footsoldier.

It was a March of madness. It threw up malice in abundance. It was a month of mendacities, mischiefs, and misgivings. Why do people descend to base lows in pursuit of power? What is political power really about? Perspectives from the March 2016 presidential primaries confirm what I have always thought: Power politics is much more about the human ego and vanity; the good of the society is secondary, an accidental consequence of a parasite unknowingly working for the host.

Machiavelli[27] imagined that politics and morals have no relationship. How then does the good of the society drive a good politician to promise and provide? Simple: by feeding his or her ego and vanity, the society gets a politician to change the course of its life.

> ....[I]t is in this manner that we obtain from one another the far greater part of those good offices which we stand in need of. It is not from the benevolence of the butcher, the brewer, or the baker that we expect our dinner, but from their regard to their own interest. We address ourselves, not to their humanity but to their self-love, and never talk to them of our own necessities but of their advantages.[28]

The beginning of wisdom for a politician is the fear of losing an election. Everything politicians do from one election to the other is to win and maintain power. Politics is a game with major and minor characters pushing for vantage positions and playing for their diverse socioeconomic and ethnoreligious interests. In 2016, we see a peeling of rich power mongers who manipulate many modern elections in the backroom. The majority voters, minor players, now feel the power in their hands to feed the egos of politicians directly. They chose Trump, on one side, and Sanders, on the other. Both candidates emerged without taking money from the major players. Trump has his money and the strong support of the right-wing base. Sanders gulped donations and support from the left wing. Some call the development an anti-establishment revolt!

---

[27] Nicolo Machiavelli, 1515: *The Prince*
[28] Adam Smith, 1776: *An Inquiry into the Nature and Causes of the Wealth of Nations, Book 1, Chapter 2*

Sanders has no way of beating the Democratic machine, not in this election cycle. Time is no longer on his side. Clinton's camp has learnt the lessons of 2008: control the party headquarters' throve of information logistics and human resources, then fight on the battlefields as if life depends on it. In 2008, Obama was able to stall and overtake Hillary by sheer marathon determination and brilliant brinkmanship. He and his team took on Clinton's machine and triumphed. She bowed and served. Obama got his mileage. It is now time for Obama to pay back in full. Hillary Clinton is ready and waiting to relish the flavor of his favor.

When the dust settles, the Republican Party will be stuck with Donald Trump, the groin-grabbing sex scandal and all. He will mobilize the grassroots of God, gospel, and guns that the party grew in greenhouses of fear and hate. The party nurtures its grassroots on a diet of tactless opinions about race and religion. With the election of Obama in 2008, these people panicked. They no longer trust the promises of the establishment. They want to see *old* America back! They want to "take back our country." Ironically, they adopted a *politically correct* banner from one candidate who openly abhors political correctness: *"Make America Great Again."*

America is great; the greatest nation civilization has known. Could it be greater? Yes. Developments bring progress. To "make great again" is a euphemism for the teabaggers' mantra: "Take back our country"! Take back what from whom… how, why? What exactly do they want back: White House? Great! In that case, the possible ascendancy of a woman after a minority male surely adds to the fear of too many swift changes.

Trump is in no way ready to be the President of the United States; he is not prepared to lead the greatest country on earth. He does not have the personality to manage the complexity of a federal bureaucracy and the intricacies of foreign affairs. He is a political greenhorn. He believed in buying big politicians to do his biddings. If he wins, if something goes badly wrong and he wins, his vice president could be the most powerful ever. Trump will be making deals and soaking the aura of his presidency. Those who want to see "old America" will not get it, whatever that means. It is simply no longer possible without another war to reverse the one that President Abe Lincoln fought.

Either way, not much will change. America is not about any one person. With Trump, lose or win, the Republican Party will be a victim of the poisoned food it cooked for Obama. Win or lose, Trump has exposed the underbelly of an organization that refused to educate its grassroots properly, a party that has identified but failed to address its lack of empathy for differences and minorities. Trump may expose his liberal self and force-feed the party a "don't-ask-don't tell" acceptance of LGBTQ and abortion under certain circumstances.

The 2016 elections may be about everything from immigration, ISIS, ObamaCare, outsourcing to Mexico, Muslims, and many more things in-between. One aspect that eludes pundits is the future elections in America. Simply stated, if the results of 2016 elections do not stump Trump emphatically, then future elections may breed worse anti-social elements. It will open the path to more meanness and anything-goes campaigning: the crazier, the better. Will the moral majority ever recover?

It is no use stargazing the future under Clinton or Trump. Looking back to past presidents, what they said during campaigns did not always happen. George H. Bush asked American to read his lips. He soon reversed. Assuming 2008 Obama had evolved from civil union to marriage of two human beings of any gender, would he have won the presidency? If then Senator Obama had planned to visit Cuba, would he have won in Florida? We may never know the exact answers to these and other what-if questions. What we know now for sure is that four years constitute a long time in politics. Things will happen. Unexpected events will demand answers.

This year of 2016 will be historic: Two New York residents will be contesting the presidency of USA. For the first time, a man and a woman will be carrying the flag of the two major political parties. Hillary will not only be the first woman nominated by a major party, she will be the first former First Lady to run for the US presidency. She will add being the first First Lady to become a senator, run for the presidency, and become a secretary of state. She may take to the White House a former two-term president as "the First Gentleman," or whatever the country chooses to call Bill Clinton.

Trump will record some remarkable firsts too: The first business mogul to become president without having ever held a political office nor served in the military. He will take to the White House a foreign-born First Lady, second only to Louisa Catherine Johnson Adams (wife of President John Quincy Adams, 6) and the first ex-professional model. Though he will not be the first divorcee in the White House, Trump will check in three marriages that produced children.

At this point, any voting American (far too many still do not vote) who has not decided for whom to vote is either not an educated electorate, or the person is not being sincere. With due respect to the candidates of other parties, the choices are clear: Hillary Clinton or Donald Trump. Nothing in the polity will change the selections of the big two. The choices of vice presidential candidates will not make much of the difference that McCain's choice of Sarah Palin made. None of the two major-party candidates will make the ill-advised choice that McCain made in 2008.

One thing is clear: too many Americans want to firebomb the federal government with a flamethrower. The right found the perfect person in Trump; the left, in Bernie Sanders. The Republicans have no other answer to tornado Trump; the Democrats are too robust to let in socialist Sanders. This throws a wrench into the field: 'Hillary is too predictable; Trump is too unpredictable.' Actually, Trump is more predictably unpredictable than Hillary is predictable! Hillary is likely to be hawkish and to the right of Obama, while Trump is sure to be hawkish and the exact opposite of Obama.

The two candidates present difficult choices for independent voters, who do not find credible choices in either Gary Johnson or Jill Stein. The endgame boils down to uniting all faithful party members to stay with the base. The far right will use the Republican Party hatred of Hillary, while the far left Democrats use the unpredictability and temperament of Trump to rally Sanders' supporters. Independent voters will ultimately follow the candidate with the political momentum and no new serious scandals after the Labor Day.

If I were a Republican, I will vote for Mrs. Hillary Clinton! That way, the party will settle down and rejig the base. If Trump wins and panders to the far right that brought him to prominence, the Tommy Tawms who want to win at the expense of others will take the party down a rough road. A dam of Democrats defending the many achievements of Obama will emerge. If the dam gives way, 2018 will be another season of shellacking.

If I were a Democrat, I will vote for Trump. Why? Unless the Congress changes colors, the Republicans will be ready on day one to impeach Hillary just for fun! The messy fight will so demoralize the party that, four years hence, stronger Republican candidates will pick the party apart and produce filibuster-proof majority and a Republican royal ready for the White House.

For independents, the choices whistle in the air. The media have helped "bigly" to thrust Trump to the forefront of national politics. He is a showman. He says things that make pundits plead to come on TV shows, spew unimportant opinions, and generate more topics for discussions. The viewing public loves to watch as the media broadcast "breaking news" from all angles. Often, when a news item is all about Hillary, videos of Trump still stream to keep expectant viewers glued.

In normal times of old-time politics, it would not be a contest between Mrs. Clinton and Donald Trump. These are not normal times. Far too many people want a new direction in post-Obama America, and it is not that Obama disappointed. Ironically, many Americans do not focus on the root of the dysfunction in Washington, DC: Congress. Trump is not doing Republicans much favors; neither is Hillary helping Democrats much.

I gave electioneering a long berth after March. This was very easy to do. Between work and Olympic Games in Brazil, there was so much to keep one busy without surfing into the shallow and annoying lakes of cable television channels. Now post-Olympics 2016 and all the dramas, I am able to steer away from the debates and the post-debate analyses. Of course, many could not escape politics. In a cave with Wi-Fi, Trumpmania will still come inside with smartphone apps! On NBC's *Saturday Night Life*, the debates are a staple.

During the first presidential debate on Monday, September 26, 2016, Trump retorted to the claim of paying no federal taxes: "That makes me smart." Hillary Clinton's campaign pounced on it. Trump backpedaled and offered that what he meant was "IF I DIDN'T" pay federal taxes (and got away with it), that would make him smart. I was no longer logging, but I wondered why no one thought of OJ Simpson's *"IF I DID IT"*?

No one is *thinking* anymore. Those who could vote early have voted and moved on with their lives. Those who have not voted listen to conspiracy theories. This is why the news of Russia hacking Mrs. Clinton and DNC's emails buzzed like normal news. Ditto, when Dr. Bennet Ifeakandu Omalu, the Nigerian-American doctor who discovered and branded chronic traumatic encephalopathy (CTE), postulated on Twitter: "It is possible she [Hillary Clinton] is being poisoned." Hillary had stumbled after the 9/11 memorial service in New York City, NY, an effect of diagnosed pneumonia. The doctor who saved her is another American medico of Nigerian extraction, Dr. Oladotun A. Okunola, a neurologist based in Morristown, NJ.

On Friday, July 22, 2016, Trump accepted the Republican Party's nomination, with the Governor of Indiana Michael Richard "Mike" Pence as his running mate. The shadow of Bridgegate had sealed the chances of Chris Christie. On Tuesday, July 26, the Democratic Convention in Philadelphia, PA nominated Secretary Hillary Rodham Clinton, with Senator Timothy Michael "Tim" Kaine, D-VA as her running mate. Tim's fluency in the Spanish language could be a factor in getting out the Latino votes, especially in Colorado and Florida.

Failed hopefuls now litter the road to the final top two. On the left side are: Senator Bernard "Bernie" Sanders of Vermont, former Maryland Governor Martin Joseph O'Malley, former Rhode Island Governor Lincoln Davenport Chafee, Harvard Professor Lester Lawrence "Larry" Lessig II, and former Senator James Henry "Jim" Webb, D-VA. On the right are: Ohio Governor John Richard Kasich; Senator Rafael Edward "Ted" Cruz, R-TX; Senator Marco Antonio Rubio, R-FL; retired neurosurgeon Dr. Benjamin Solomon "Ben" Carson; former Florida Governor John Ellis "Jeb" Bush; former Virginia Governor James Stuart "Jim" Gilmore III; New Jersey Governor Christopher James "Chris" Christie; former Hewlett Packard CEO Cara Carleton "Carly" Fiorina, former Senator Richard John "Rick" Santorum, R-PA; Senator Randal Howard "Rand" Paul R-KY; former New York Governor George Elmer Pataki; former Arkansas Governor Michael Dale "Mike" Huckabee; Senator Lindsey Olin Graham, R-SC; Louisiana Governor Piyush "Bobby" Jindal; Wisconsin Governor Scott Kevin Walker; and former Texas Governor James Richard "Rick" Perry.

A casual observer may think that the other candidates for the presidential elections have fallen by the wayside with the over 1,500 candidates who filed a Statement of Candidacy with FEC. One thing is to file, another is to meet the various state requirements and deadlines that qualify a candidate or a party to be on a state's election ballot. These dizzying laws for ballot access vary from state to state.[29] The rules show why only major political parties can afford to qualify across all the fifty states and why independent candidates face uphill tasks. A serious new party should soak up all the other contending interests into a major third force and provide Americans with a needed and viable alternative to the big two. Else, these parties are mere sour spoilers.

The major candidates for the 2016 United States presidential election were:

Democratic: Hillary Clinton/Tim Kaine
Republican: Donald Trump/Mike Pence
Libertarian: Gary Johnson/Bill Weld
Green: Jill Stein/Ajamu Baraka

Other presidential candidates who made it into more than fifteen percent (15%) of the general election ballots include Darrell Lane Castle (Constitution Party), Rocky De La Fuente (Reform Party), Evan McMullin (Independent) and Gloria Estela La Riva (Party for Socialism and Liberation). None should get up to 1% of the total votes cast, but the measurable impact of these parties collectively may easily tilt the title away from the frontrunner, especially in consequential states.

---

[29] https://ballotpedia.org/Ballot_access_for_presidential_candidates

Postscript

Trump won. Unbelievable? Sure! Even with all his braggadocio, Mr. Trump barely believed it. It was believable to those who had followed his tawdry Twitter tweets, the cuddle of America's major media networks (drivers of television-viewing habits), and the mean mood of Middle America—home of the angry white males and the faithful females who vote the way of their men.

America delivered another surprise of the new millennium. Who seriously thought that a freshman senator named Barack Hussein Obama would cruise to victory twice over two Republican royals? Backtrack: who said that America would vote for Ronald Reagan? What about choosing George W. Bush (GW) over the establishment-solid Al Gore, a sitting vice president, and John Kerry, an experienced senator and decorated Vietnam War veteran? Before Bush, 43, a few believed that an upstart and scandal-ridden Bill Clinton could defeat politically solid and sitting President Bush, 41.

Those who follow politics closely see no surprise in Trump's triumph. I reminded my Facebook friends who were wondering why and how the Republican Party could produce and hoist Trump on America:

> *This is a party that wanted to change the Constitution so that
> an Austrian-born, Kennedy-family-connected, and nanny-
> bumping muscleman named Arnold Schwarzenegger could
> run for the presidency of USA... just because he won an off-
> season governorship contest in the great state of California!
> Yes, the same party of Lincoln that situated Sarah Palin a
> heartbeat away from the nuclear codes! Now, you think this
> same Republican Party... with all the odious Obama-phobic
> obstructionism... is not that cracked? No, I think not!*

On Friday, January 20, 2017, America welcomed President Donald John Trump as the 45th President of the United States of America. He defied everything, everything that in normal times would have sunk the presidential hope of any normal politician. Trump is not an average politician; he is actually not a politician. Trump stepped into a world that is wider than his 24/7 Twitter account. His vast business experiences will help, but the presidency is more than moneymaking deals. The presidency is about the greatest military power that could dunk the world into a nuclear cloud. Fortunately, the Congress exists; it will not roll over and allow any harebrained hashtag to hatch into policy.

Secretary Hillary Rodham Clinton will remain a good grandmother. She got a raw deal from four flanks: President Putin's Russian KGB, James Comey's FBI, Senator Bernie Sanders' refuseniks in Michigan and Wisconsin, and "the basket of deplorables: [t]he racist, sexist, homophobic, xenophobic, Islamophobic"[30] — those whose votes she was never going to get anyway. Still, she may have the last laugh. Time will surely tell.

---

[30] Hillary Rodham Clinton, speaking at a fundraising event in New York City, NY on Friday, September 9, 2016

Trump is good for Tommy Tawms, emotionally. He got *their* beloved country back from a long list of *deviants and diversities!* Alas, much like the coming and going of Obama, Tawms will be disappointed when all the curtains of Trump era fall into place. For minorities, Obama was a great spiritual success, an upliftment that instilled pride in the American democracy. He did not boost their socioeconomic security exclusively, and he did not advance their political power greatly.

The triumph of Tommy Tawms will not be a total hollow victory, but it will not bring the expected goods. The country will not change course considerably. There will be no mass deportations and no walls will seal the southern border with Mexico. No one is going to start a nuclear war, hopefully. No one will crash the economy for the heck of it, nor enrich Tawms disproportionately. All things will happen as they have happened: in cycles. The poor, as Jesus prophesied, will remain amongst us.[31]

The Trump era may do more in mobilizing many citizens to vote and to run for offices, just as Obama's win unleashed the forces that eventually made Trump. The voter turnouts in elections are abysmally low for America. It is thus ironic and troubling that some states make pronounced illegal efforts to discourage minority voters, instead of encouraging all Americans to vote. On the other hand, those seeking elected offices depend so much on the power of political parties and the media. Person-to-person campaigning and small neighborhood rallies no longer hold. The use of social media worked for Trump, but the novelty is wearing thin.

---

[31] Matthew 26:11

Trump's win affected familial relationships and friendships. Many may recover after two Thanksgiving dinners. No one knows for sure how Trump will change American politics. One thing is obvious: Trump will certainly change America's political culture. In the end, America will soak a trail of toxic policies while Trump and friends sail into the sunset of life, richer but not better off for the decision to step into the DC swamp. The Washington, DC swamp is legendary. It is a pigsty. No one steps into a pen of pigs and exits with a sweet smell. 'Drain the swamp' is a great desire, a romance. Reality is different. The stump of Trump v. Mueller[32] (Russiagate) will tell generations yet unborn of the great American gamble with Donald Trump.

Long after the four or even eight years of Trump, as long as American public institutions remain strong and Americans have virtuous faith in these institutions, the country will triumph. Not many will say the same thing about the temporary triumph of Tommy Tawms, nor about the abracadabra that aborted the dream of an American first female president. American society is changing, and it will continue to change. The triumph of Trump may delay the changing trajectory that started with the miracle of Barack Obama, but it cannot stop the changing shades of American society. Of course, these political permutations cannot stop the intrusive and extensive effects of the social media on the global real and cyber (virtual) society. These cyberological changes are unstoppable; we must study and ground the issues.

---

[32] Robert Swan "Bob" Mueller III, the sixth Director of FBI (2001 to 2013) and special counsel for Russia investigation, also known as "Trumpgate."

Cyberology proposes to study the Internet in all its ramifications. Cyberwar, an aspect of cyberology, made Russiagate possible. Russia meddled. Whether Vladimir Putin approved the meddling is another story. American intelligence agencies have determined that Russian hackers had a finger on the scale for Trump and skewed the process against Clinton. The Congress has sanctioned Russia. It is not clear if a definite collusion between Trump's campaign team and Russian hackers happened. Still, fingers point to a certain conspiracy involving WikiLeaks and Russian oligarchs close to Putin. The Mueller investigation will reveal the level of real collusions, not just conspiracy theories.

With all the Ivy League education of many who suffered the humiliation of Trump, from *Crooked* Hillary to *Lyin'* Ted, it took North Korea's Kim Jong-un,[33] to give Mr. Trump a stickable nickname: *Dotard* Trump. Then again, folks would have considered the jab ageism … even if the aged did not act the age.

Trump will leave his footprints on the sands of American existence; the depths are dependent on many factors that only a soothsayer can speculate. It is either Americans buy the abracadabra, the *yooge* hocus-pocus of our elections, or wake up and strengthen the union. Many eyes have seen the darkness of divisions. Many Americans do not like what they see. One can poke out a pinkie and posit that it will be a rough ride to the end. Saddle up!

---

[33] Kim Jong-un is the Chairman of the Workers' Party of Korea and the Supreme Leader of North Korea (2011-present). He is the second son of Kim Jong-il and the grandson of Kim Il-sung, the founding leader of North Korea (1948-1994).

****

One year into Mr. Trump's presidency, I have an answer for my friend who wanted a reminder on any country that writes checks to Americans: Russia! Russian oligarchs have written fat checks to Trump's businesses over the years. In the 2016 elections, they bought a big bony fish they cannot chew and swallow. Meddling in the sacred US elections is a step too many. It may bring down many prominent people and prove to be an unbeneficial venture. Buying into Mr. Trump's trademark is one thing; messing with the elections in these United States of America is another.

If the intention of the Russians was to corrupt the American electoral system thoroughly, the contrary is obvious. Institutions work better than individuals do. Russia and America will survive both Putin and Trump. This is the great justification for forms of government: "whichever is best administered is best." It does not matter much over time who is at the head and or what games s/he played to get to—and remain at—the top; the abiding respect for the foundations and traditions of orderly representative governance is best.

Also in America versus Russia, the Churchillian truth triumphs: "You can always count on Americans to do the right thing—after they've tried everything else." Regardless of the Trumpian "bait which they… eagerly swallow[ed]," enough Americans will see the light at the other end of the tunnel of trickery and refocus on doing the right thing, not by force but according to the commands of the Constitution. This is the bottom line: noble institutions, not individuals. Nothing else trumps.

Index